Narcissistic Abuse

How To Recognize Covert Manipulation, Outsmart The Abuser And Get Your Life Back

Theresa Evans

Table Of Content:

Introduction:
This Is A Wake-Up Call

I'm someone who has encountered abuse and neglect in her life from many different angles. Emotional abuse is something that we will all have to face at some point.

My abuse started sweetly, as most do—I was so overcome with love for my partner that I failed to recognize the warning signs. My mind chalked up all the red flags as something I could ignore, something in my periphery, a fluke that would be solved. It was because of that ignorance, that willingness to turn a blind eye that I became trapped in the cycle of an abusive relationship. It took years for me to get out of that relationship and doing so was almost as difficult as actually being in that relationship knowing that what was happening to me was wrong. I felt happy at first and I tried to drown out the feeling of dread in the pit of my stomach with the feeling of being in love, of being loved—or so I thought.

The truth is that my dependence on my abuser was being set up from the very beginning, and it meant that the process of escaping that circle of abuse was only so much more difficult for me and took that much longer to recover.

The pain that I went through for so long, and the pain that I still go through today from the aftershocks of those experiences, is exactly why I wrote this book. This book is a wakeup call! This is your sign, no matter how much you needed one or thought you didn't. This is the sign that you need to start thinking about your relationship, the power dynamics between you and your partner, and how the relationship is making you feel. When we get involved in a toxic relationship, it can feel natural to want to push our emotions by the wayside for the sake of caring for our partner. But this is a set-up by your abuser to get you in the habit of not caring for yourself as much as you should. This leaves your defenses down and allows for the abuser to get into your head and directly manipulate your thoughts, feelings, and actions.

This book is for people not only in an abusive or toxic romantic relationship but also for people who are in a bad position or relationship with a platonic partner or with a member of their family. Abuse can come from anywhere and being prepared for that abuse is difficult. This book serves to help you be prepared and know more about the tactics that an abuser might use on you, and how you can defend yourself against them.

Chapter 1:
The Dark World Of Emotional Manipulation

There are several different kinds of abuse that are utilized by abusive and violent people against their victims. There's physical abuse, psychological abuse, and emotional abuse. Psychological abuse and emotional abuse are, at many points, one and the same, so both will be addressed as one compact sensation with its own definition. Emotional manipulation is the result of emotional and psychological abuse when the abuser is in a place of power where they hold information over their victim, or they simply have the metaphorical upper hand at all times in their relationship.

There is a certain amount of power imbalance and, to some degree, a manipulation which is normal in a relationship and not necessarily unhealthy to either person. Someone might manipulate their partner from time to time in a white lie, trying to protect their partner from having their feelings hurt or from potential harm. While this is an act with pure intentions, it is still manipulation and should never be accepted as a total norm in any relationship.

Couples fight and say bad things to each other. They may act petty and do petty things to one another from time to time, but it's the growth from those petty things that sets an unhealthy relationship apart from a normal, healthy one. No matter how manipulative a partner, friend, family member, or boss might be, the relationship has the capacity to be normal and healthy if the manipulative person in that relationship is willing to grow for the sake of themselves and the other person in the relationship. A true abuser will never grow because the proper incentive to do so will never be there. The only incentive that an abuser will take to grow, and change is something that deeply affects them, not something which affects someone besides themselves. Abusers lack empathy and care less for the feelings and fates of other people than normal people might.

In general, if your partner seems to try to pay attention to you at all times, they aren't abusive to you. If your partner seems more involved in changing you than they are open to the possibility that they need to change instead, they might be abusive and/or emotionally manipulating you. A partner who dedicates a large amount of their time to fulfilling you and helping to meet your emotional needs and desires is not very likely to be genuinely abusive or manipulative of those emotions. An abuser is, put most simply, someone who is unwilling to commit to the emotions of someone else. To an abusive partner, there is nothing more important than their own feelings and their own goals. How they get to those goals is ultimately unimportant, and they're willing to use anyone and everyone to get where they feel they deserve to be. This drives them forward and encourages their manipulation of others.

In some bizarre form of manifest destiny, the true abuser does everything in their power to get to what they feel they deserve using everything and anything they can. The more time you send around your abuser, their true goal may become obvious. But even if they know that you're realizing you're in an unhealthy relationship, the actual manipulative behavior probably won't change much. Abusers are aware that the way they act is wrong but don't really care. They only want to change in a way that will help them achieve their goal, and this often means that they'll have to hide their methods to some degree, especially in public, where people might try to take the victim away from their abuser. And especially the public field is where they apply their dark art of covert manipulation.

Covert manipulation is the kind that most abusers will use against their victims. This is the kind of manipulation that snakes under the skin of the victim and turns them against themselves before they even truly realize it. Covert manipulation occurs when the abuser goes out of his or her way to make it seem as though they are a good person, simply trying to help their partner.

Here is the other difference that lies between a healthy relationship with a sometimes-manipulative person, and an abusive relationship. Someone who is manipulative accidentally or without realizing manipulates without malice. They don't act the way they do because they like to inflict pain on their close ones, people who they care greatly about. A true abuser, however, may not care in the slightest about these people. Those that the abuser should hold dear are, in the end, just steppingstones for the abuser to take what they believe they deserve: power and control over whoever they want. This is the desire they manifest in their relationships. An abuser makes up for the power they lack in their normal life by taking excessive control over their relationships by manipulating everything their partner, friend or family member thinks, says, or does. An abusive or toxic person will exorcise any and all power they have over dominating their partner in every way they can.

A manipulative person might accidentally say

something controlling because they lack awareness. An abuser doesn't lack awareness of the cruelty of their actions, but they don't perceive themselves or their actions as wrong. More often than not, an abuser views themselves outside the rest of the world. They view themselves as special, separated from the meaning of a moral compass. There is no "cruel" or "merciful," no right or wrong or black and white, only what they feel they deserve and what they believe they have to do to gain the power they think they deserve.

This feeling of entitlement not only drives the abuser to do cruel things to their victim, but also to act cruelly to other people around them who they may not even know well. Sometimes, an abuser will only put on their charming persona to people who they want to keep close to them. Weak and vulnerable people who the abuser can use to project their fantasies of power onto. Most abusers are, in some way or another, fairly narcissistic, and have a large web of dependent people who they can dominate and take control of.

In many cases, after one of their victims is able to get out of the relationship, they don't mourn the loss for very long. The main reason an abuser might put on a genuine show of grief or sadness may be because they are around someone else who they plan to take for their next victim. This cycle will often continue with many different people being used by the same abuser to fulfill their obsession with power and dominance.

Generally, abusers are predictable in the way that they treat their victims, their prey. Abusers are kind and charismatic at first—they tell their partner they love them and take them to beautiful places, give them gifts, and shower them with praise. After the connection between the abuser and the victim has been solidified, however, the whimsical nature of their relationship might quickly wear off. The compliments that were once kind and sincere are now backhanded if they come at all.

The victim is manipulated into believing that they

shouldn't hang out with their friends, especially male friends, out of courtesy to their partner who has treated them so well. This praise and showering of affection early on works against the victim as the relationship progresses. When the two are out in public, the abuser might make a show out of belittling or teasing the victim. Although the teasing seems like a playfight, the exchange is usually the abuser making sure that their victim understands where the power in the relationship lies.

This is how most power dynamics in abusive or toxic relationships function. The abuser has the upper hand, if only slightly by physicality or something else equally irrelevant. However, this isn't the way that the abuser achieves true power and control over their victim.

Physical abuse and negligence aren't at the core of the abuser's arsenal—the main tool that the abuser will always use against their victims is emotional abuse. The bullying and the teasing in public, although seeming harmless, even caring to some people, is just a show of who's really in control. The victim doesn't speak out or argue back for fear of raising a public fuss or worse, angering their partner. Because the victim is too afraid to argue back or stand their ground, they become more deeply trapped in the cycle of abuse while the abuser hammers home more and more that there can only ever be one person in control of the relationship. It's this little cycle within the larger cycle of abuse that traps the victim further into the idea that they will never be able to take the upper hand from their abuser in the relationship. In a healthy relationship that was able to grow, a victim of manipulation would be able to take the power swiftly away from the manipulative personality. With a highly abusive person, however, this is unfortunately much less likely to happen within reason.

So, where does this leave victims at the end of the road? Unfortunately for victims of an abusive relationship, the road to recovery is often just as difficult, if not more so, than the actual steps to get out of the relationship in the first place. In a sense, victims become addicted to the abuse and to their abuser. The person may be all they know, their only partner, or the (seemingly) closest person to them. Many abusers cut their victims off from as many outside sources of affection and attention as possible, doing two things in the process.

Firstly, the abuser tricks the victim into thinking that their partner is simply someone worried about being able to protect their loved one. This is endearing, but ultimately not true. Secondly, and more importantly, cutting off the victim from their friends and family leaves them with only on social contact which is still entirely intact—their bond with their abuser. That means that even long after the victim has realized that they're being abused and has left, they may come back to their abuser for that feeling of familiarity. Even though they understand that they were being abused, that their partner or friend or this person who was in their life treated them very badly, they need that "fix" of nostalgia, to feel something from their past life, no matter how bad that thing may be. Similar to addiction, we long for things that may hurt us, or worse. This very rarely dulls the ache in our hearts for it.

It's up to the victim to best understand how their abuser can manipulate them. Learning about your abuser and trying to understand how they manipulate you and abuse your emotions can help not only to prevent you from being tricked by them, but it can also empower you against them. Being able to take control of one part of your life, how much you know and what information you're taking in, can lead to you taking back other parts of your life and in your relationship. Where your partner may be trying to dominate and control other parts of your life, being able to take back even one can be the beginning of you waking up and taking your life back from your abuser.

This wakeup call isn't just for people who are in dangerous or toxic romantic relationships. Toxicity can take many different forms throughout our lives. Whether it be a friend who you feel is taking advantage of you or a family member that you feel suffocated by, or even a boss who you feel may be abusing you emotionally or taking some other part of your life away. A toxic relationship can crop up in any corner of our lives. Our work lives become affected by these relationships; our social experiences become relatively limited and we become disconnected from other people because of our abuser.

In a platonic relationship, of course, the abuse takes on a slightly different form. Where in a romantic relationship, the abuser might justify their abuse and manipulation by saying that they love you or that they're envious of whoever you might have been in contact with. A friend might argue that they feel betrayed when you become close to someone else, or that they're just looking out for you. Although the intimacy of a sexual or romantic relationship is lacking in a platonic one, your abuser will use the same core tactics on your feelings in order to get just as close to you so they can do the same things to keep you close. Even a relationship with your family member will, in the end, be similar to a toxic relationship with a romantic partner. Although the identity and the relationship between you and your abuser will change, the way the abuser will behave will stay essentially the same, no matter how close you are with your abuser. Your abuser, no matter the actual context of your relationship or how the two of you are connected, will try to maintain absolute control and dominance over the victim.

Whether the victim is alone or with friends, the abuser wants to make sure that they can achieve two main goals at once; assuring to the people connected to the victim that their victim is safe and not in need of aid, and making sure the victim always knows that the abuser is the dominant one in the conversation. The teasing and the picking, the subtle jabs, and the back-handed compliments that you may have thought were normal or benign, are signs of worse public treatments once the victim get used to these smaller instances of verbal abuse.

This is how abusers get their victims and keep them—by starting them off with small instances of concerning behavior. When the negative behaviors are introduced, the victim is often already snagged by their abuser in a whirlwind of infatuation. Because the victim already believes that they're truly in love with their partner, they're more willing to overlook small infractions, they turn a blind eye to normally concerning things. By the time the feelings of infatuation have worn off, the victim is already used to the abuse. When the victim is used to a small amount of abuse, the abuser introduces more and more of their evident control. This is the dynamics of emotional abuse.

Chapter 2:
The Psychology Of The Emotional Abuser

The mind of the abuser is based around desires and the willingness of the individual to fulfill those desires. Their manifest destiny, or their instinct to do what they want regardless of moral restraints that would stop a normal person, takes over and they do anything within their power to achieve their goals. These goals usually have a lot to do with control, feeling as though they have power over some part of their life. Even if it's impossible for the abuser to control a particular part of their life, they dedicate their time and energy to at least feeling as though they do have some semblance of control. It's in this desperate delusion that a manipulative abuser is created—someone aware of their flaws and violent tendencies, but utterly unwilling to do anything about it. They lose their empathy and their pity for other people who have troubles in life. They're people with tunnel vision, only really focused on the future they feel that they're fated for, the future they think they deserve. They think that the future they're owed is going to be achieved by exerting their will on other people. Their victims act as the vessel for the admiration they so desperately want to have. Therefore, they pick out people who are generally kind, soft, and loving. They need people who will be kind to them, especially when they might not deserve it. They need someone who is the opposite of them. While the abuser is cold and cruel, they attach to empathetic people who will be warm to them regardless of how terribly they've been treated by their abusive partner. They believe in second, third, fourth chances, perhaps to an unreasonable degree.

However, as kind as the victim of abuse may be to their abuser, no matter how forgiving they are, this goodwill is lost on their abuser, on their partner. Even if the victim is unconditionally loving toward their cruel partner, their abuser physically doesn't tend to understand this kindness. The abuser is manipulative and was raised as a child used to being manipulated. This is all they know, the nonverbal language they speak best—so of course, they'll speak it to everyone else, even if they're undeserving of the cruelty in the manipulation. There's no difference to them between a cruel person and a kind one, as long as the person can get them to the fate, they think is in store for them. They'll take advantage of all these people, no matter how kind or unkind they've been to the abuser. The abuser doesn't care about goodwill. There's no positive karma for people who treat the abuser well. The relationship the abuser has with this other person is already probably set in stone—the abuser is willing and able to manipulate every person they meet to achieve their goals. There's no point in investing emotionally in anyone unless there's something physically in it for them. Any reward which is anything other than purely physical might as well be no reward at all.

The abuser is someone who has mastered deception and manipulation, they understand how the human mind works and does everything in their power to exploit the weaknesses of everyone they meet. Although they appear to be benevolent when they first come into contact with their newest victim, they'll quickly lose their interest in them as soon as their victim is properly attached to them. It's this way that the abuser keeps their victim wanting more from them. The abuser will start out treating their victim kindly, giving them lots of affection and compliments at every corner. However, once the victim becomes used to this praise, the abuser quickly revokes it.

Now that the victim has become used to the affection and is being deprived of it suddenly, they think that they're doing something wrong now, that they need to try harder to win the affection of their partner back. In reality, the partner never intends to give their victim that full attention ever again. This game of desperation and almost-compliments keeps the victim trying to latch onto the abuser and get closer to them so that they might receive that praise they miss so much. When the victim is so fixated on getting back onto the good side of their partner, they're suddenly able to block out all the negative parts of their partner's personality. Everything "wrong" about their abuser, every negative part of their behavior, is now more likely to be chalked up as the victim's fault. They fall into that habit of blaming their partner's shortcomings and cruelty on themselves. They believe that this dip in praise compared to when they first met is their fault and that they're charged with pleasing their partner so that they can feel that praise again. Again, remember that the abuser doesn't actually feel any sympathy or pity for their victim. They're purposefully doing this to keep their victim in a loop of blaming themselves for the abuser's actions and emotional abuse. They're even proud of themselves for doing this to their victim. They only view this abuse as something impersonal, just another step on the path the abuser is forging for themselves. Their victim, and keeping their victim under their thumb, is just their way of getting what they want.

In general, the abuser is made up of three groups of

traits—psychopathic, narcissistic, and Machiavellian. These three groups of traits are referred to as the dark triad. This triad of groups combined make up the ultimate abusive, manipulative partner. Many abusers will have some blend of these three groups, but each of the triad has their own list of traits for the individual type.

The first group of traits is the psychopath. This is someone who was born without empathy and has a very hard time connecting to other people. They feel nothing like guilt or remorse when they hurt people, and genuinely don't understand these feelings coming from other people. The idea that they should care about other people and their feelings when there's no physical or immediate payoff for them is absurd and unthinkable for them. Because the psychopath lacks so much empathy, this set of traits lends itself to abusive, manipulative behavior. You might know someone with psychopathic traits if they seem to lack human connection or lack an important amount of empathy for the people around them. If the person sticks out in the middle of a crowd because of their lack of social ability, they may be a psychopath or have psychopathic tendencies.

A psychopath isn't someone necessarily violent or inherently evil. Quite the opposite, psychopaths tend not to be very physical. If they do hurt others, it's through their cold behavior and manipulation of the other person's emotions. A psychopath is someone most likely to hurt others, even though they may not understand the gravity of their behaviors. The way they act may be harsh and cruel, but a true psychopath doesn't always act this way out of spite or malice. They act this way not because they have some kind of vendetta against their partner of anybody else, but because manipulation is almost always the path, they'll take to get what they want the most—the feelings of power and control over others. A psychopath might manifest their control over you the most literally of the three negative groups, dragging you away from your connections and making sure you can't get the positive emotions from them or from anyone else. This is how the psychopath controls their victim—making the victim feel cold. Getting them away from the connections that matter most to them, so that the self-esteem and confidence of the victim rests in the hands of the psychopathic abuser, and no one else.

A psychopath shouldn't be confused with a sociopath or someone raised in an environment that caused them to act without sympathy or guilt. A psychopath is someone who was born with these traits, although their upbringing can amplify them. A psychopath is someone who simply acts in self-interest because it's what makes the most logical sense to them. They have a very difficult time relating to other people because they literally don't see the reward in doing so. Overall, this kind of person is characterized by cold behavior and turning a blind eye to the wants and needs of others for the sake of preserving their goals. They're often cruel in their actions and don't care about how other people react to them. The reactions of others don't matter, no matter how they're related to the psychopath.

The second of the dark triad is the narcissist. Someone with a narcissistic personality may be the easiest to spot because it's in a narcissist's blood to shout from the rooftops how proud they are of themselves. A narcissist is someone who believes themselves to be special or of some higher quality when compared to other people. A narcissist will do anything to achieve their goals because they feel that they are special and that there are higher things in store for them. They might believe that they'll someday rule the world, or they might just think they're better than the surrounding people.

Narcissists often adopt a harsh worldview when it comes to other people—they put a lot of emphasis on the status quo and the popularity of themselves. They believe that popularity and being loved are key traits of a good person, and the attempt to commit acts of kindness and goodwill means little to them.

Many people with NPD or narcissistic personality disorder don't realize that the way they're acting is wrong. Narcissists, unlike psychopaths, are not created from genetics. It may be possible that there are some people who are genetically more likely to develop narcissistic traits, but the personality itself is determined by the surroundings and influences in the early stages of the individual's life. Usually, a narcissist is created when the guardians or other people around them in childhood spoil them or replace actual affection with material goods. The child then equates power or rank with these material items, and they grow up with this mindset close to them. As they grow into adulthood, this way of thinking affects the way they interact with the world around them, including their friends and family. As an abuser, the classic narcissist has the compulsion to manifest their pride in public and in private in their relationship. All the public teasing and the jabs in private, as well as the boasts to their victim about how much power they have, how good they are at what they do, how smart and how kind they are, this is all chalked up to their narcissistic personality traits.

If you know someone personally in your life, whether they be your partner or a friend of someone entirely out of your personal circle, you may be able to tell more easily than some other traits. Because narcissists so often tend to broadcast things about themselves to the world and to anybody who will listen, it can be pretty easy to pick up on someone with a narcissistic personality, even if they aren't technically a clinical narcissist.

Someone who tends to brag about their accomplishments more than a normal person, someone who tries constantly to put others down for the sake of elevating their own perceived status, or someone who's obviously willing to hurt other people's feelings just to make themselves feel better, may be a narcissist. Someone who genuinely, deep down believes that they have some kind of special path laid out for them or that they have some secret the rest of the world is below understanding, is probably pretty narcissistic.

A narcissist is someone you can recognize from a mile away, but the hidden traits of the narcissist are often much deeper, and much more disturbing than the traits which are displayed on the outside. A narcissist, while annoying on the outside, is just as abusive as a psychopath to their partners and loved ones, if not more. A narcissist is so wrapped up in their own narrative that they cast aside everybody else in their life, no matter how close they are to them or how much the person should normally mean to them. The people in the close circles of the narcissist are only there as placeholders, just empty spaces, and blank slates for the narcissist to harass and abuse. The verbal and emotional abuse from a narcissist is often more gratuitous than the psychopath. While someone with psychopathic tendencies might accidentally injure someone's emotions because they were too wrapped up in themselves to pick up on their effect on someone else, a narcissist takes joy and pride in ruining the self-esteem and confidence of other people. Seeing people crumble emotionally is often what makes the narcissist's day. In the context of an abusive relationship, this means that your narcissistic abuser is most likely to increase your pain and emotional suffering. They're sadistic and it feels good to them to watch their victim fall apart and know that they're the one directly responsible for it. The absolute power that they can hold over you is terrifying, and the narcissist is proud of the way they make their victims feel.

The third and final part of the dark triad is the Machiavellian. Machiavellian abusers are people who don't care about the feelings of anybody around them, especially not their close ones. They take their relationships for granted and often look at the world around them through a very harsh lens. They don't feel as though they owe anybody anything and don't like to take any kind of advice or aid from anyone either. They're cruel and remorseless and often consumed by self-interest. By definition, a Machiavellian personality is not someone who chooses to be manipulative. They release their ownership of their negative and harmful behaviors. They believe that they are simply meant to be manipulative, that they were born with the destiny before them.

There are mainly two different kinds of Machiavellians—low machs, and high machs. A low mach is someone who manipulates others but doesn't try to force the answer they want out of others. They believe that the people around them are essentially good by nature, and they use that benevolent nature to their advantage. You may know a good mach if they manipulate others slowly over time. They don't infringe on the personal space of other people immediately. As an abuser, a low mach would be a partner who is abusive to you but seems generally passive. They're agreeable and let you do what you want, but they make you feel bad for doing so. This slow manipulation builds up against the victim until they give in and let the abuser do what they want. This is a win for the low mach, allowing them the reign that they wanted for so long. Their manipulation isn't immediately abusive to you—they understand what they want and are patient with getting it.

A high mach, on the other hand, will force themselves on you and are much less patient in getting what they want. They believe that humans aren't so good-natured, and they don't feel empathy or pity taking advantage of anybody around them. The high mach is the kind of person who assumes that everyone is just as harsh and cold as they are, and they treat their relationships accordingly. They force you to think the way they want you to by guilting you and making you question your perception of the world. The way that a Machiavellian, low mach or high mach, will abuse you is the most manipulative of the three. The narcissist and psychopath will cut you off from your loved ones and your most meaningful connections, but the Machiavellian will make you feel awful about trying to do something about it.

The narcissist traits might make you fall in love and want to stay around your abuser, but the emotional manipulation of the Machiavellian traits will keep you around for a long time. The Machiavellian is the kind of person who makes you fear for your sanity—while the psychopath and the narcissist traits dominate their victim emotionally, the Machiavellian will force their victim, their loved ones, into psychological warfare. Gaslighting is an excellent example—a victim of abuse being tricked into questioning the way they perceive something that happened. For example, if a victim thinks something happened to them that was unfair or blames the abuser for something they did, the Machiavellian traits of the abuser contribute to them spinning the story on its head, making the victim wonder if the way they perceive the problem is real. Once a victim of abuse loses confidence in the way they perceive and understand reality, they become more likely to simply accept the reality as the abuser offers it to them. This lets the abuser have a direct effect on how their victim responds to things and a direct line to how the victim thinks. When the abuser has all the control over reality as the victim knows it, the abuser has full control of the victim psychologically as well as emotionally.

It can be difficult to understand when you, as a victim, are actually in contact with any of these dark personalities. There are many ways you might be able to tell if your partner/abuser is manipulating you or showing signs of the dark triad. A psychopathic personality will show itself through a cold personality—they're cut off from other people and want to do the same thing to you. You might be able to pick out a psychopath or psychopathic behavior in your partner depending on how willing they are to separate you from your other relationships. Regardless of the relationship you have with the other people outside your partner, a friend or a family member or anything else, the psychopath will try to make sure the only person you have contact with regularly is them.

A narcissist is also fairly easy to pick out, but the darker side of a narcissistic partner might be a bit more hidden beneath the surface. Narcissists are very aware of their persona, the way that they appear to other people around them. Because they're much more in touch with how they appear to the world and fit in within it better, they're less likely to entirely cut off their partner from their other loved ones. Instead, a narcissistic abuser is likely to make sure their victim spends most or all of their time with them. A narcissist is characterized by being consumed with pride and ego, so they want their victim, as well as other people in their life, to pay attention to them almost exclusively. They want their victims to be part of their cycle of abuse, their cycle of having to pay attention to them and be an emotional sponge for their boasting and emotional abuse. As a victim, you'd be able to pick out a narcissist fairly easily based on these traits. A partner who is overly prideful or who tries to force you to back down socially and make way for them is a narcissist.

A Machiavellian may be the hardest to pick out, as they're something of a cross between a psychopath and a narcissist. While a psychopath is usually fairly obvious with their cold personality and the way they often stick out in a crowd, and a narcissist will usually let you know their personality and their behaviors as if they were something to be proud of, Machiavellians are usually more careful about how they appear to the people around them. They're aware that their behaviors can get them in trouble, so they're especially proficient at deception and manipulating not only people but the way they're perceived by those people. You'll be able to more easily know if you're with a Machiavellian if they seem disconnected from their empathy. Not necessarily for lack of understanding others, but just out of lack of motivation to understand.

This is at the core of almost all abusers. They simply don't care—about your feelings, about their own feelings, only about their motivations and their goals, and the things they think they're owed. This sense of entitlement that abusers have in common becomes their reason for their abuse. They're all willing to do anything to get what they want, and their partner, their victim, falls by the wayside in the meantime.

Chapter 3:
Feeling Insecure, Weak And Jealous But It All Started So Promising

Unfortunately, emotional abuse can never be a victimless crime. There always has to be an abuser and a victim when it comes to emotional manipulation. It's a social defect, an ugly underbelly of society. Without any kind of manipulation in our world, the order of things would fall apart rapidly. Unfortunately, there always has to be someone there to take the fall. However, there's a certain kind of person that a manipulator will be drawn to.

Abuse of any kind is never the fault of the abuser alone. While there needs to be a victim for every crime, that doesn't mean that the crime is excusable because of this. The victim is just that, a victim who has unintentionally become the partner to someone destructive and abusive. However, there are many things that make a person more likely to become a victim of abuse. For example, empaths and narcissists are almost always together in some way. Narcissists, people who always need to have someone giving them attention, are usually around empaths, people who soak up emotions like a metaphorical sponge, and who are always willing to listen to the complaints or boasts of other people.

Empaths, and generally people who are sympathetic to a fault, are vulnerable to emotional manipulators of all kinds, regardless of where they fall within the dark triad. While an empath doesn't choose to be so receptive to the emotions of others, there's something in them that compels them to be overly kind to others. They're gullible and easily led along by other people, which leads to them getting hurt often. This is exactly the kind of person that the abuser preys upon—someone unsuspecting and easily tricked who can be guilted and manipulated into a relationship.

With this kind of person by their side, the manipulator can do as they please and have someone there as a personal stepping stone for their goals, and they usually don't really have to worry about interference from their partner. Usually, empaths and other very sympathetic people are too concerned with how they interact with others and taking care of their partner to be able to take a step back and consider if they feel good in their relationship. The same thing applies to a family member or friend. If they can pick out somebody in a crowd who looks meek or overly submissive, they'll cling to them and won't let them go.

Often, empaths or people who are otherwise just very kind and unsuspecting were raised by people who, in a way, traumatized them from the time they were small children—usually by their parents. Many adults who are submissive in personality and have a hard time manifesting their will on others come from a family who was always exerting their own will onto their child. This kind of narcissistic parenting can introduce the child to a cycle of abuse that it can take their entire adult life to get out of if they do at all.

A narcissistic parent or family member can severely damage the way that a child grows up and interprets the world and the people in their circle as an adult. A narcissistic parent will essentially do anything they can to live vicariously through their child—they haven't yet become emotionally stable enough to have a child, so they try to get back what they missed out on through their own child. This can include many forms of abuse, such as using their child as a simple extension of themselves. This can include referring to their child as a miniature version of themselves, referring to their child as them or vice versa, or trying to get their child to relate to them in any way they can. Even if the child is too young to grasp certain things, the narcissistic parent may try to rely on them as if they were an equal or a friend. In a sad turn of events, the parent will often actually be the one who needs to be supported, as they're not emotionally or psychologically sound enough to care for and protect a child of their own. The narcissistic parent has expectations and goals they set for themselves, even unreasonable ones, and they project the way they want to achieve those goals onto their child.

Just like a narcissist manipulates their partner or friends and family, a narcissistic parent manipulates their child into being a steppingstone for the parent's end goal. The key thing to note about this kind of parenting is that, unlike most parents, there was no shift in priorities when they became a parent. Instead of their priorities shifting from themselves to their child, the priorities of the narcissistic parent stay the same. They're still mainly concerned about themselves and how they're going to get what they want. Their child is either an impediment or a blockage to them, or a tool in order to achieve whatever it is they think they deserve from the world.

On the other side of the spectrum, many narcissistic parents might pressure their children by putting them on a pedestal. Instead of pressuring their children to be just like them, they project their own ego onto their child, causing the child to grow an ego of their own. Through this treatment, the child becomes just as egotistical as their parent, believing that they're also owed anything and everything they want from everybody. When they don't get what they think they deserve, the narcissistic parent may even step in and defend their child, believing their child could never do any wrong. They associate their child with themselves, thinking that an infraction from their child makes them a bad parent. So, they'll do anything to avoid admitting that they, or their child by extension, did anything bad or wrong. As the child grows up with this treatment, they grow up to be a full-blown narcissist in the real world, treating people the way that they were allowed to treat others as children.

Because their parent was never concerned with teaching them right from wrong or how to properly communicate with and respect others, the child grows up with a skewed and faulty perception of how the world works. The child grows up to become an abuser, and then needs someone who they can let off all their narcissistic steam too—enter you, the victim of their emotional abuse. While the narcissist was abused themselves in their childhood, this doesn't make their own abuse of other people acceptable or ok. While it's difficult for an adult to break the narcissistic habits, they've been developing for years, it isn't impossible by any means. There are some cases in which the child of a narcissistic parent can become the exact opposite of that parent—they become exceedingly submissive, desperately living out their lives hoping that they can please the people around them. Whether that be a boss or a family member or their manipulative partner, they begin to absolutely dedicate themselves to serving others in the hopes of receiving the praise they never really got from that narcissistic guardian.

Some children will get genuine affection from their guardians—not all narcissists are evil, cold-blooded, and cruel people. Many narcissistic parents genuinely care for their children. However, many narcissistic parents will only offer their children this genuine love and praise as a reward for something. Whether it be natural good looks, good social skills, good grades or good performance in extracurricular activities, the child is trained to believe that praise and affection are something that you must earn from even your parents, your family. They grow up with this mindset and go on believing that they have to go above and beyond to achieve even basic respect from their peers and loved ones. In a healthy relationship, both partners will love and support each other through their shortcomings and mistakes, as long as both people try to change for the better. In any kind of narcissistic or otherwise abusive relationship, that love is a reward/punishment.

When the victim of abuse does something good or "right" for their partner, they receive praise as a reward. If they do something "wrong," like disobeying their partner, they're trained not to defy them again because they're immediately deprived of that love from them. This only further solidifies the understanding of how relationships work for the victim, and it intensely damages their social skills.

In adulthood, we begin to see the flaws in our parents, our earliest role models. Because we're distanced from them and can look at them with a more critical eye, we can start to see if we did have abusive or narcissistic guardians.

Your parents may have been abusive to you if they cared a disturbing amount about your appearance. Abusive and narcissistic parents see their children as little more than an extension of their own body and personality, so they want their child to be just like them. So, if their child is "ugly," the parent might treat their child really differently based on that perception. By that same point, children under narcissistic parents lose most of their voice, so to speak.

The child of a narcissist doesn't get asked how their day was, how they're feeling, what they want for dinner, because their parent doesn't actually perceive them as an individual with own wishes and needs. To a narcissistic parent, the child is little more than a small carbon copy of themselves, so there's no point in trying to learn more about or connect with their child. This can make the child grow up with little grasp on self-esteem and their own ego. While they may grow up overly secure, just acting to everyone else the same way their parents acted to them, most children who are treated so dismissively will grow up not understanding how to connect with other people. Someone else genuinely caring about them and their opinion of foreign to them, putting a serious backlog on their social skills and their ability to start the conversation.

If you think back on the way your parents saw themselves when you were growing up, think about how much they compared you, as a child, to themselves. Even when you couldn't properly articulate your feelings as well as a teenager or adult, a narcissistic parent might compare you to them so that they can feel successful. After all, they're their own inspiration. Any narcissist will idolize themselves in everything they do, no matter how well they actually do it. They view themselves as the epitome of a human, in whatever job they're doing. Being a parent is something they do best, the way they see it, and they can become irrationally angry if you criticize the way they parent. So, even as an adult it may not be a good idea at first to bring up any complaints or criticisms.

A narcissist can be turned back into a normally functioning person, but it can take a lot of time for them to realize that they genuinely have a problem and need help. In general, when you look back on your childhood and you find that you were cast aside and neglected for the sake of your guardian's pride and emotions, they may have been narcissistic parents.

The abuse that we receive in our early years often transfers over into our current relationships—if there's some negative behavior we first came in contact with while we grew up, it's likely that we'll run into it again if we enter a toxic relationship. Most abusers are similar, and they use similar tactics to keep you around them. However, for abuse victims, there are many things that keep them around their abusers that aren't even technically their doing. While they might have a hand in it, or amplifying the effects, there are some things that abuse survivors might run into that crop up again when they're around a new abuser.

One of the most prevalent of these afflictions that an abuse survivor can often face is the Stockholm syndrome. The Stockholm syndrome occurs when a victim develops some kind of genuine bond with their abuser. This happens in many kidnapping cases—the person who has been taken will form a bond and attach themselves to their captor. Although it might sound strange to someone who's never experienced anything like the Stockholm syndrome, it can be very confusing for an abuse survivor to simultaneously be aware that they're being abused and mistreated while also feeling a connection with their abuser.

Because most victims of emotional abuse tend to be very submissive and empathetic, it's very easy for them to form a bond with just about anybody, even people they've never met. Simply being human can be enough camaraderie for someone empathetic enough to bond with someone they've never spoken to. It's in this way that a victim can become empathetic, or even try to be friendly with someone they know is abusing them. They probably know that their abuser is someone who's been abused just like they have, and they try to appeal to the fear and anger that their abuser feels from that abuse earlier in their life.

However, they also know in ways that even if the same things happen to them and their abuser, the result would be relatively the same. Maybe the victim had a support system after their abuse that their current abuser didn't, or if it was just the nature of their abuser to let the abuse harden them. But the victim must accept that they and their current abuser have very little in common.

Their abuser may even try to connect with them too, pretending to break down and open up to them. This façade makes the victim believe that they're special, that they're the only person who can "get through" to the good part of their abuser. Their unwavering belief that all people are good allows them to believe that their abuser can be changed for the better. While this is an endearing idea, it is not true. It's only a ploy by the abuser to make the victim feel more connected to them, to keep them closer in their abuse circle and further prevent them from slipping away.

While the abuser usually doesn't start this cycle of trauma-bonding, they pick up on it quickly. When it happens they are able to manipulate it to their advantage. Even if the abuser did, in fact, suffer through the same or similar abuse that their victim did, it doesn't change the fact that the abuser is willing and able to manipulate, lie, and cheat where their victim is morally sound to do those things. This is the barrier between the victim and the abuser, even if suffering seems to bind them together.

This is the delusion that a lot of victims suffer from—because two people suffer through trauma, they are both yearning for the same things, at the same time, for the same reasons. As humans, we look for connections in the world even when they do not exist. This is especially true when we try to find some companionship in people, we may not actually have anything in common with. Abuse victims in particular often develop a tendency to attach to people who they feel an attachment to, but they have little common ground with. Victims of abuse are likely to attach themselves to anybody they can, and this includes their past or current abusers. Victims might also attach to their abusers because they fear what might happen if they stray too far. Because victims who were once abused as a child or in a past relationship often have issued with attachment and loneliness, they can have a very hard time letting go of people.

They can become convinced that their identity is intertwined with that of their abuser. This can also partially be at the hand of the abuser who was also likely a victim of abuse, who has experience of how that attachment can feel. They want their victim to latch onto them and never let go. So they manipulate their partner into feeling like they'll lose themselves as a person if they move away from their abusive partner. The victim might fear that they'll suffer an identity crisis or some kind of spiritual death. A phenomenon in which the victim feels lifeless or as though they've lost all purpose in their existence, if they're left alone without a partner. So they let themselves be manipulated and abused because they can at least feel as though they have someone. In addition, the abuser might commit acts of kindness or praise every once in a while, in order to keep their victim closer to them.

In a way, an abuser sees their victim like their prey while hunting. They want to lure them in, start the relationship off comfortably, making sure the partner is infatuated and not likely to leave. As the abuser gets more used to having their victim around, and the victim becomes more used to being with their partner, the relationship becomes sourer. The praise becomes sparser, with compliments fewer and farther between. The victim has to be more desperate if they want that same attention, so they latch onto their abuser and do everything they can to please them. This is often the case with children of abusive or narcissistic parents who have spent their formative years desperately trying to earn the attention of their parents.

In the end, many victims of abuse will always have that endless feeling of loneliness in their head. The feelings of being abandoned and losing a loved one through their childhood or from other instances of past abuse will stay with them. And so being in a new relationship can be a quick fix for a victim who's desperately searching for the attention they need so much, that they were deprived of for most of their younger life.

We would like to think that we can change all the people we meet for the better. Whether it be helping a loved one with a bad habit or getting someone who has been abusing us to see the better things in life, to see that they can change and be a better person. It's easy to develop this delusion, especially as someone who has been abused in the past.

I thought this way too—I thought that while I was with my abusive partner, they would slowly change into the perfect version of themselves that I saw within them. To be blunt, it didn't work—my partner continued to manipulate me, and I saw that they didn't care enough about me or about anyone else to seriously consider changing themselves or their personality for good. Abusers see themselves as a gold standard, usually—they don't see how someone below them could even dare to think they need to change. The simply see it as an insult that their victim is trying to change them or suggesting a way for them to change. There is no such thing as growth when it comes to a classic manipulation—because they already perceive themselves as perfect. To them there's nowhere to go but down.

We would all like to think we can make a huge impact in the world and in everyone we know. However, this isn't the case all the time. In order to move forward, you have to let go of the hope you have to change the people you love. Not everyone will want to change, and not everyone will even think they should. In the case of abusers, you cannot change people who want to hurt you and prey on you. They exist alongside you not to help change you for the better, but to change you into a more subservient, submissive version of yourself. Once they can do that to you and fit you into the version of yourself that they can most easily manipulate and take advantage of, they have no interest in you as your own person.

While a relationship with your abuser might start out fine, it will always end in pieces. Your abuser will simply move on to another victim, someone more submissive and eager to please them, and they'll leave you there to fend for yourself. Your abuser is never interested in your personality. They're interested in how they can use you to their advantage. However, you can learn to avoid this ending if you can see the signs of an abuser before they can ruin you.

Chapter 4:
How To Recognize The Signs Of Emotional Abuse Before It's Too Late

An abuser will do everything in his or her power to make sure you feel restricted. He will slowly take away all your freedom over the long or short term. The more time you spend with your abusive partner, the more likely that they'll find more and more ways to keep you from running away.

Immediately after entering a relationship, you might notice that your partner starts to isolate you from other people. Whether that be your friends or your family, your work friends and other colleagues, or anyone else around you, your partner will begin trying to guilt you into staying away from them. They'll set ground rules that limit how much you can go out, how much you can talk to your friends. They will guilt you into following their rules and they will claim "they're only doing it because they care about you".

Abusers will try to capitalize on the fact that you know they were abused or hurt when they were younger. They know you'll pity them and try to connect with them. Acting out of this pseudo-vulnerability makes them much more capable of cutting you off from other people. Regardless of whether that abuse actually affects them, they use that status to make sure you cut them more slack. You will give them more second, third and fourth chances, than you would give to someone else when it comes to setting these restrictive rules.

They take advantage of the guilt you feel for them and they use it against you, making sure you're unlikely to go out of your own accord to hang out with friends. Being around other people allows you to get second and third opinions, fresh perspectives on your problems and relationships. This can be a trouble for an abuser who only wants you to be able to process your own judgments and theirs. The opinion of someone who exists outside their jurisdiction is a problem, so they try to limit how much time you end up spending with them. Everyone else in your life is an unknown variable for the abuser, and they can't handle the thought that there's someone out there telling you what is and what isn't good for you.

This can also apply to a lot of social media. Your partner might try to monitor what you do and post on social media and might try to place some ground rule about inspecting your phone from time to time. The abuser wants to know what you're thinking and who you're interacting with at all times, so they can monitor what information and what perspectives you're experiencing. These invasions of privacy will very rarely go both ways, of course. The abuser doesn't want to have their information or privacy invaded by anyone, let alone their victim. This can come off as hypocritical, and it is. If you feel comfortable, call them out on it as soon as you see these rules being set. Only confront your partner about these things if you feel safe doing so. The worst thing in an abusive relationship is to try to get your partner to confess to something or change their behavior and only end up getting hurt.

Regardless, you can't stand by and watch these things happen. If you notice this going on, and you feel like you're being restricted in what you can do and who you can talk to and you didn't consent to, bring it up with your partner. A partner who is abusive and trying to take advantage of you might respond with another way to guilt you, making you feel bad for questioning them and their rules.

They may become angry with you for defying them or even questioning them, or they may fake sadness and grief, tricking you into thinking their feelings have been hurt. Regardless of how they react, try to get your partner to respond to your questions. Make them specific; "why don't you want me to hang out with this person? Is there a specific reason for this rule?" the questions should be easily answerable. Even if they are easily answerable, a classic abuser won't answer them anyway, because the truth is that they have no valid reason for forcing you into these rules.

The true reason that they're forcing it on you is that they want to cut you off from the rest of the world, to limit your perception of the world to only them. Of course, they can't tell you that. If your partner can't answer any questions in a straightforward way, they might just be using or manipulating your emotions.

Abusers will start these rules and acts of control in a way that appears affectionate and kind. They'll start out these rules as precautionary measures, just decorum that they'll play off as not meaning anything, just done out of fear or concern for your safety. As the relationship progresses and the abuser becomes more comfortable asserting their dominance around you, however, these rules will become more restricting, colder, and stricter. The technicalities of these rules will become harder to ignore, as your abuser closes down the already small circle of people, they originally allowed you to communicate with.

The point of doing this is so that the abuser can get you to trust that they have ultimately kind and selfless goals, so you're less likely to object to them. By the time you're uncomfortable enough to think about confronting them, the power dynamic of that abuse has been established. Your abuser already has their methods wired deep in your brain; deep enough to manipulate you into turning a blind eye to your own abuse and manipulation.

The kind of control they try to exert over you can become much more apparent as the relationship between the victim and the abuser progresses. Some victims, in a sense, train themselves to look away from what's in front of them. They chalk up the shortcoming of their abuser to their own failures and misdeeds. Where the abuser of the victim might come short on something or express frustration, the victim can even try to cover for them and take the blame for themselves. Even if this seems like something you do for the wellbeing of someone else, the abuser is manipulating your sense of civic duty and kindness to paint you in a negative light. The abuser wants you to feel like everything you do is bad, everything bad that happens to you or around you is actually your fault. This kind of thinking that the abuser tries to force into your head is their way of controlling you. They force you into a state of shame where it's very hard to get out of.

When you already feel as though most of the terrible things that can happen throughout the day are actually your fault, it becomes exponentially harder and more embarrassing to try to speak up for yourself. We often feel as though we don't even deserve the chance to speak up for ourselves. This is massively damaging to our ego and helps the abuser to break us down over time. By the time the abuser is satisfied, their victim has no will to do anything on their own terms. The abuser teaches them that it's simply best to let them do the talking and that there's no benefit in questioning them. The abuser trains their victims to feel stupid and worthless all the time, preventing them from speaking out against what they might find to be abuse.

Some victims notice abuse when it happens to them, and are conscious of it, but the resulting silence is about the same. However, the early awareness of what's happening can be the thing a victim needs to prevent the worst from coming. This worst might take the form of emotional or verbal abuse becoming physical, or the anger in the relationship worsening. A victim who understands that what they're going through is abuse is fairly rare, and one who maintains that clear understanding throughout an abusive relationship is even more so.

Usually, as a relationship progresses and the abuser makes up more and more strict rules for their partner to follow without question, their way of thinking tends to transfer over to the victim. The victim tends to think the way the abuser wants them to more and more as time goes on. All the things the abuser does to change the way that the victim functions in the world around them slowly begins to pay off. When an abuser cuts of their partner from the outside world through social media and other methods, the victim has little choice but to listen to what their abuser has to say.

Even if they start out aware of the abuse and they still stay with that person, there is no compromise that can be made between the two. No matter how much the victim might think they can change the abuser, no matter how much you might think you can still turn their life around, you can't.

The abuser's personality is set in stone until they themselves take the initiative to change it—something which doesn't happen very often. Even when it does happen, it usually doesn't last long. It's more likely that your abuser is only pretending to try to improve themselves so that you stay with them longer, making sure you invest in them more. The more of yourself you put into something or someone, the harder it is to let go of them. Under this train of thought, it's nearly impossible for a victim who has been trying to "save" or change their abuser to truly let go of that challenge.

Unfortunately, not everyone can be changed by a new face and a positive attitude. The abuser is just as able to change as anybody else, but they must reach out with sincerity and be willing to take the hand of someone neutral. Not only is it astronomically rare for an abuser to bare their true self, but you, as a victim of their abuse, are not neutral to them as a person. Much in a way that a therapist can do for a person what their friends cannot, you cannot help your abuser or anybody else in the same way someone with a neutral, critical eye could.

While the abuser sets up dominating and controlling rules for you, you might see their armor start to crack a bit—you'll begin to see the real person inside the manipulation. Abusers tend to get their partners to let them help with just about everything; after enough time, the victim stops trying to do things for themselves and they depend on their abuser for just about everything. Once in a while, you might see their genuine reaction to the victim's early refusals to help, even if that help is genuine.

What an abuser lacks the most in the world is the ability to let things go, let you go, and allow for things to happen naturally around them. Abusers are most often produced from environments in which they were deprived of any control over what happened to them or the people around them. Whether they witnessed a family tragedy or felt helpless to stop something that happened in their earlier years, this desperation for a handle on their life and relationships transfers almost seamlessly over into their adult life. They need to feel as though they have a strong grip on everything and everyone they interact with. So, when you refuse to let them help with something, it can anger them severely. They can become frustrated and massively upset with you.

However, they can also become very afraid and scattered. This is the genuine reaction of the manipulator, the abuser, losing control of something and not understanding why. They might genuinely panic or freak out instead of becoming angry at first. They don't really understand why you wouldn't just let them do this for you, even if it is all in the name of making you dependent on them. At first, you can't reasonably know that. You should assume that they're just trying to be nice and help you, and yet you're resisting. It's something the abuser doesn't understand, and that lack of insight terrifies them like nothing else in the world. It can be scary for anybody to come into contact with something they don't understand, but the way that we all react to this situation dictates our character. So, when you are in a situation within any relationship, try refusing their help, and see how they respond. Do they calm down, take a step back, apologize for intruding or allow you to do whatever you were doing? This indicates someone who not only is ok with not being in control all the time, it indicates that the person trusts you to a degree where they allow you to act on your own free will. They understand that you know what's best for yourself. This is a healthy partner, and likely a healthy relationship if that trust remains throughout the entirety of the relationship.

An unhealthy relationship, however, is indicated by a partner who becomes upset or distressed when you try to refuse that help. They don't understand why you wouldn't just rely on them, and they don't take into consideration your comfort or whether you know what the best decision is. The only thing that matters to them is that they can be in control comfortably and make sure they have a handle on the situation at all times.

Even if you protest, they don't really care how you feel about it, because they simply assume, they have the highest understanding of the situation. They might even become angry with you, lashing out and accusing you of being callous, cold, or even— ironically—untrusting of them. They can be frustrated by your decisions and frustrated by the fact that you're even choosing to make those decisions on your own instead of deferring to them. If you're with someone who's frustrated or even angered by you choosing to make your own choices on your own terms, that the relationship will go sour quickly if it hasn't already become immediately bitter.

In many cases, the abuser will even try to literally track you, wherever you are. This is just one other way that abusers cling to any semblance of control and dominance they can wring out of you, out of the world. An abuser will either make sure you always have some kind of app on your phone with location-tracking abilities, or they'll make sure you always have on some setting on an app or device which allows them to know where you are at all times. They'll try to make up an excuse for this unacceptable and invading behavior—it might be trying to guilt you by accusing you of thinking lowly of them or thinking that they're untrustworthy.

They may try to pin the real blame on you, pointing out any male acquaintances or friends you hang around. Many abusers spin any male attention to be your own fault and paint it as a promiscuous experience. Of course, the same can be said for female abusers as well, who will point out that you supposedly flirt with women outside your partner or something else within that realm of logic. Or, they may even guilt you by explaining their own abuse. This is not only an attempt to empathize and falsely connect with the victim in the hopes for more pity. But it's also a way for them to try to justify their own trust issues and need for control.

The abuser pushes off their shortcomings and issues on someone else without having to waste their time addressing them. That's more time where they can monitor you and make sure they know where you are at just about any time of the day. This can be a scary thing to consider, being in a relationship and having to be afraid of whether your partner approves of where you are and who you're talking to.

Generally, the most important thing about being in

a toxic or abusive relationship is not being able to get out of it after a long, hard-fought battle. It's being able to go into a relationship and understand when you should head out before you get in too deep. Being able to logically think your way through this kind of situation can save you potential years of your time that you could have spent having everything you thought you knew about yourself broken down. Seeing the signs in front of you that something just isn't right between you and your partner—or, mainly with your partner—is the first step to being able to dodge possibly the most dangerous bullet ever. In many cases with abuse victims, being able to learn from your experience with abusers can even save your life.

Being able to look at your abusers from your past and apply their behaviors to who you think might be a potentially abusive partner can help you make out what it is about them that puts you on edge. Many of us get this feeling in our bodies, we feel something just isn't sitting well. That gut instinct we feel around certain people can tip us off as to who we feel safe sticking around and who we should probably ditch. Take a look at the abusers from your past and consider what it was about them that really made you afraid of them—what stuck out about those people in particular? It might be a certain trait of theirs, a tic they had or an especially bad habit that left some kind of impression on you. It doesn't matter what it is about your past abuser that sticks out in memory; the important thing is that the thing that sticks out to you from the past is also usually applicable to the present.

Most abusers are alike in many ways and share many of the same personality traits. Statistically, it's likely that something you recall from a past case of abuse will also be present in your current abuser. Be able to think about the similarities and differences between your past abusers and your current one. If there aren't any exact similarities between the past abuse and the abuse you might be facing at the moment, why are you able to compare them?

Even if there are no exact parallels between people,

they likely have some kind of feeling about them which is similar. All abusers make us uneasy if we're able to see through their tricks and their façades. It's being able to accurately see through them which is always the most difficult.

When you are able to pinpoint what makes you so uneasy about a person, you have to then decide what to do next. The most important thing at that moment if you're actually with the partner is that you can't betray what you're feeling. Whatever emotions you're going through, once you're settled on wanting to get away from this possibly abusive person, the abuser will do everything they can to pick up on those feelings. They want to sniff out your feelings so they can capitalize on them and make you feel as small as possible. If you can avoid having your feelings found out quickly, you can also avoid the following manipulation of those feelings that manipulative abusers are so skilled at.

So, what can you do once you've figured an abuser out? Once you have your emotions under control, you have to think about what you need to do next.

How are you going to get out of the situation? Even if you aren't actually with the abuser, it can be very difficult finding a way out of a relationship that's in its early stages or technically hasn't even started yet. If you're with your abuser, it's often best to simply ride out the interaction and explain that you think it might be best if you didn't see one another again.

If you and your partner are very new to one another, they probably won't have their hooks in you so deep that they would feel comfortable openly guilting you or forcing your hand yet. So, you can probably get away with normal means of separation and rejection if the relationship is fresh or very new.

If you're living with an abuser and you fear that if you try to break up, things could become violent or physical, it might be best to force your way to some safe location. From that safe location, make sure that there are other people who are there who make you feel grounded and protected. From there, do what you need to do without living in fear. There are many public service groups who aid and shelter victims of domestic abuse, people like you who might live in fear of what their partner might say or do to them if they were to disobey.

It's from these people who are now running from their abusers that we have to understand our own strengths and how important it is for us not to miss our chance. When we first meet our abuser, they seem so incredibly kind and sweet. We want to be with them forever, and we feel like nothing in the world could keep us apart. As the relationship becomes older, that feeling rots and falls apart, becoming a strange and uncomfortable mix of fear and dread for what might happen to you if your partner becomes too upset and lashes out at you. Living in fear of our partners, the people who we are supposed to love and who are supposed to love us is saddening. But a relationship where you are forced into a corner and made to be subservient or afraid of your partner is not love, it's abuse.

It sometimes takes victims of that kind of relationship until after they've left to realize that. When we're with people who always treat us this way, we accept it as the norm that we just have to get used to over time. This unfair treatment of our bodies and feelings is something we're told we just have to accept. And we often don't even understand that this is wrong until we leave and see people treating us as equals. When we have nothing to compare abuse to, torture becomes acceptable and even negligible.

There are different phases that the abusive relationship is split into. These phases dictate how a relationship like this plays out, how the abuser does everything in their power over time to crack down the victim to the depths of their most basic format. Over the development of the relationship, the way abuse looks shifts and changes to fit the wants of the abuser, what they need from their victim. Of course, when an abuser first enters a relationship, things look fine. When we look at our partner and our relationship through rose-colored glasses, we often miss the red flags which are so obviously swaying in front of us. Being able to remove this hopeful lens and truly look at the relationship for what it is, seeing what's wrong with it and thinking about what we can do to react to it, can save us many times down the road.

Chapter 5:
The Phases of Emotional Manipulation

The most important part of an abusive relationship might be the first moment within it—the first contact you make with your abuser. This first contact you make may be the most important part of that relationship. The way that we make first contact with a person and the way that an abuser makes first contact with a person are massively different, and this shows most of all when we first meet them. That first stage of that relationship is led by that first touch, the first impressions of both parties.

As a victim, when we meet someone, we think about what they're thinking and what that might lead to. As people who have a tendency to live in fear and anxiety for most of our lives after being in the cycle of abuse, we look for a way to escape from almost everywhere we find ourselves. When we're trained as people to be afraid of our partners, we don't have the positive experiences with other people, which would assure us to act more calmly.

However, we look at new people we meet as just that—as normal people, more or less. Normal people grow up meeting new people by spending time around them and checking for themselves if they get a good feeling from that person. This is how we're used to interacting with people, and we treat most other people we meet like non-threatening presences. We understand the world around us as relatively safe and we connect with people out of a desire for security and companionship. We check if their "vibe" is one that we connect with.

Most normal people have a sense of character and are able to read people for their true characters easily. Some people are a better judge of character than others, but most normal people have in common that they spend their time understanding someone better simply through practice. Spending time with someone you know better is the fastest way to get to know them on a more personal level. It's through this repeated interaction that we become closer to other people. That interaction forges a new relationship with them over time, and we get to know them even better. This is the cycle for most normal people, socially.

Abusers, on the other hand, very rarely act this way when they first meet someone. When an abuser first meets someone, they try to sniff out the weaknesses of other people. They look at a person as someone who could act as a steppingstone or another pawn for them to get where they think they need to go. They use everyone they meet and they think there's something in it for them, and that mainly includes potential victims for a relationship. When you first meet them, they'll analyze you to try to find out how you function. Abusers usually have a lack of understanding of how people function, so they're mainly focused on understanding people they meet on the most literal level.

This is where abusers locate empaths, in particular—highly sensitive people are usually able to be picked out of a crowd, especially by manipulative people and abusers. Empaths are usually very reactive to meeting new people and will show their emotions on their faces very plainly. They react expressively to the feelings of other people, and the abuser understands this and uses it to their advantage by trying to draw emotional responses out of them. When they do so, they confirm to themselves that they're meeting someone very empathetic, likely to try to sympathize with them whenever they can. In addition, the abuser will try to see if they can gauge how submissive you are when the two of you first meet.

As you spend more time with them, they will offer you more opportunities to defer to them and let them do what they want instead of offering you that opportunity. The more you allow them to exert their will over you at these opportunities, the more the abuser is assured that they can do so farther into the relationship. This entire set of first meetings between the abuser and their victim is the set-up for abuse. They groom their victims, trying to scope out what part of their personality they can take advantage of and to what degree.

When they come into contact with a new person, they immediately begin to look at that person as either someone expendable to their grand plan or someone who they need to keep around for at least the time being. Those who he does keep around are the victims who are often the most empathetic, the most kind to them, the most willing and able to see the good in people and the good in bad people, in particular. Seeing this potential for good things in all people, no matter their past actions, is good and kind.

However, not being able to balance this kind lens with a sense of realism and what the person is likely to do of their own volition, can end with you getting hurt by that person. The same person who you may have thought you could save at one point, could end up being your undoing, your new abuser. They can turn out to be someone who manipulates and uses you for a large portion of your life in the future, a portion of your life that's incredibly hard to fight your way out of. Being able to just look at everyone you meet more sensibly can be your answer. Dodging the potential for meeting a terrible and manipulative person by developing your ability to be cautious around new people, instead of either blindly latching onto them or blindly avoiding them. Picking and choosing who you associate, instead, can be a much more positive solution.

After you make that first important contact with your abuser, and they decide you're someone they want to keep around for their own sake, they'll initiate the second phase of their plan. This phase is often referred to as "love-bombing," the infamous phase in which the abuser showers their victims with affection and praise and essentially induces a high in the victim.

When we first enter a relationship, we enter the honeymooning phase of that relationship, in which we experience elation pretty much every time we're around that person. Our new partner is put on a pedestal in our eyes, and we can't stop thinking about them. We romanticize just about everything they do, right down to the way they move and breathe. This first infatuation phase happens because the new partner and a new relationship introduce a lot of dopamine into our system.

This dopamine, a neurotransmitter often associated with rewards and risk-taking, floods our brains when we think about or interact with that new partner. This is what infatuation is, chemically speaking. The dopamine floods the brain over and over again and this heightened level of the chemical leads to extended and heightened feelings of giddiness, joy, elation, and excitement. This is the feeling of falling in love when we first meet our partner and enter a serious relationship with them. That feeling can last a long time, and the abusive partner knows how to take advantage of it. When we're right in the middle of this honeymooning phase, the abuser will love-bomb us by showing us lots of tender affection.

In a way, this softer version of their normal beginning praise and attention offsets the dopamine flooding our brain, but the abuser is also keen on how most abuse victims think and react. Large, over the top shows of love can be frightening at first, especially to someone who's afraid of attachment or being left behind, so the abuser pulls back.

Instead of these massive shows of love or infatuation on their end, they introduce the victim to flowers, handholding, gentle and soft ways, they show affection and love. In addition to this softer side of the new partner, they know how to make the abuse victim feel special as well. They'll introduce parts of themselves that are vulnerable, even secret, assuring the partner that they've never told anyone else these things about themselves. They pretend to bare their heart and soul to their partner, in an attempt to get their trust almost immediately—and it usually works.

While this act of vulnerability usually earns the trust of their newest victim, it also ensnares them into thinking that their new partner can be saved, helped, turned around down the road when the relationship begins to turn sour. When the abuser starts to act out, the victim is under the impression that they do these things and act sourly because of the damage they might have endured when they were younger. The abuser sets the precedent when the relationship is still good and pleasant, revealing some damaging truth to you beforehand. It helps them to garner sympathy from you. You want to help them and try to heal them as best you can, especially if you're someone who considers yourself an empath. This is the other reason most abusers will try to pick out an empath as their newest partner and victim—an empath is most likely to connect to them and their story, whichever story that is. When the abuser presents themselves as something like a victim of abuse in their younger years, they develop a kinship with their victim. The victim will usually reciprocate the feeling, as they're usually trying to forge some kind of bond with the people they meet anyway.

Someone who has probably been abused before is going to try their hardest to connect to people who have also endured abuse before. Therefore, the abuser has the means and the ability to forcibly connect themselves and their feelings to those of their partner, who is likely an empath—someone who feels a heightened connection to the emotions of others. After that connection is made, it's hard for the victim to separate from the other side of the connection on their own. The abuser has made room for themselves to act out and begin abusing and more brashly manipulating their victims. They feel more able to now, as they've established themselves as someone who can connect with their partner on a deeper level than most other people.

After that precedent is established along with their connection through trauma, the victim is compelled to give them more chances, to offer them more help. They're convinced that their abuser is simply misguided, just misdirected and in need of help. They're more than willing to outstretch their hand, feeling the pain of their partner, and try to give their partner help. The victim, like I've said before, can develop a bit of a hero complex—they believe that because they weren't able to receive the help they wanted when they needed it, they can be the saving grace of other people who are being abused or going through a hard time.

Ultimately, the abuser will use this optimism against the partner, which will keep the victim of their abuse closer to them as time goes on. The more strongly the victim believes they can save their partner, the less likely it is that the victim will be able to leave of their own volition. To them, if they leave their abuser behind, they'll be giving up on them and the cause they had been dedicating themselves to. In reality, this is exactly what the abuser wants out of their victim—any reason for them to want to stick around and be helpful to the abuser. The more the victim is willing to help, the more subservient they tend to be when the victim plays them right.

The next phase might come as a surprise to most victims who are coming right out of the honeymooning phase of their new relationship. The part of the abusive relationship that follows this phase full of praise and love-bombing is the exact opposite—the devaluation phase. This is the sadder part of the relationship where the partner starts to draw back all of that praise and excitement, they had given you for so long. They start to replace the praise and the intimacy you had with them with strict rules and backhanded compliments to break you down and make you feel worthless.

In normal, healthy relationships, what comes after the honeymooning phase is the opposite of that rush of dopamine. The feel-good chemical which had been flooding the brain for months, even years, dries up back to a relatively normal level.

Because dopamine, along with most other neurotransmitters, can be chemically addictive, we get used to that rush of dopamine that we had when we began the relationship. We want to ride that high forever, and so the crash afterward is just that much harder. The emotional low after the honeymooning period is where most relatively short-term relationships will come to an end because the two people will start to want to be around one another less and less as time goes on.

As they have this falling out, they get into fights more often and generally feel less and less in tune with each other. The high of infatuation and the elation of wanting your happy ending fades and you're faced with a flawed human in front of you. This revelation is jarring to people, and they usually can't help but feel more than a little disappointed. Hence, the two separate and see other people, for the cycle of elation and disappointment to perhaps repeat. The emotional low in a normal relationship is healthy—it's just the hormones in the human brain going back to a normal level.

Although it can feel as though you're drained, waiting out the emotional low will allow your brain to adjust to the new level of dopamine and other neurotransmitters. Your emotional responses to the person will also become calmer and more moderate. Your connection with that person becomes less infatuation and more actual intimate human connection—this is where "true" love actually begins.

In an abusive relationship, however, that infatuation was manipulated by the abuser to make the victim think that their elation was how the relationship should always be. That level of elevated happiness and elevated reaction, in general, is set as the standard for the two people by the manipulative partner. Then, after that connection is built and the victim is made to feel responsible for the abuser, the abuser takes back the kind things they had done for them. The intimacy and the vulnerability that the two had shared is erased, and a lot of changes happen between the two people. Where there was once kind, gentle gestures of love, the abuser now shows their "caring" nature by setting rules and restricting the victim. They withdraw their affection from you, make you feel like less of a person. The frequent texts and charming surprises slow or halt entirely, and their interactions with you might become colder, more isolated. They give you the cold shoulder, ignore you and your efforts, and treat you more like an inconvenience than a partner.

That connection you might have felt you shared through trauma or through the issues the two of you shared may feel like it's vanishing. In the place of that vulnerability, the abuser suddenly has this massive cold wall between you and them. They seem distant and like they don't want to do much with you, like go out or have dinner. The cute moments you had with them where you really clicked stop. They might even make it seem as though they feel sad, alone, frustrated, angry about something. They close themselves off from you and from other people, and you feel pressured to do the same for their sake. This is where the victim falls for the abuser's ultimate trap, one that's been laid out since the beginning of the relationship.

Because the victim already feels as though they and their abuser are connected through trauma, hardship, or something else intimate that the abuser revealed to their victim, they also feel like they have to suffer with the abuser. They think that they should sacrifice their social life or their happiness because it seems that their partner is being forced to do the same.

Because they feel like the intimate connection from before has been lost, they also feel that they have a responsibility to rekindle that relationship now with some other form of camaraderie. Alternately, the victim might feel like this colder version of their partner has been created by something the victim did. They might feel like they've been doing something wrong, not listening well enough to their partner or not doing something expected of them. They want to right that wrong, and so the victim doubles their efforts to help their partner, further investing themselves in that relationship, even though it's tearing them apart from the inside.

This hero complex that the victim has, and which has been developing with their partner for some time really comes into effect now as they do everything they can to please their abusers. When their partner seems upset or is ignoring them, the victim feels responsible for that. They feel like everything bad that happens to the both of them is somehow their fault—and the abuser knows this. They're aware of the effect they're having on their victim because they've had it intentionally set up that way since they first began interacting with each other.

From the moment the two people met, the abuser knew exactly how to ruin the positive feelings of their victim and how to get rid of them with little to no mess for them to clean up afterward.

That mess is also known as the discard phase. This is the part that hurts the most for the victim, as they may finally realize that the relationship and the connection, they had been building up inside their head doesn't actually exist. The love and responsibility they felt over caring for, protecting their partner, wasn't reciprocated. This is where the damage is done in the long term to the victim of the abuser, as they reel and have to take in that they weren't cared about at all during their relationship after all. Coming to terms with the fact that your relationship was actually hollow and wasn't filled with the love and compassion that you have thought was inside it, is incredibly hurtful for the victim in question.

After that realization on the part of the victim, they'll often get caught in the cycle of abuse where they want to leave and know that they should. But they keep getting drawn back in over and over again until they either find the courage to leave for good, or the abuser simply discards them for their next victim. As a victim, you come to the crushing conclusion that you were never seen as a human being with feelings and thoughts—you were just a vehicle to get closer to what they wanted.

The minute you didn't obey them or do as they asked, you become worth less and less in their eyes. Someone who you thought was vulnerable with you, and who you felt very personal and vulnerable with, turns out to be someone just trying to hurt you for their personal gain.

However, the abuser will very rarely discard their victim of their own volition. They usually want to keep their victim around for as long as possible, squeeze every last bit of "use" out of them as much as they can. When the victim understands that they're being abused, they might try to leave the relationship almost immediately. Unfortunately, the victim—an empathic one, in particular—will still likely have some kind of attachment to their partner. They still feel the need to help them, even if they also want to leave and distance themselves from that emotion. This need to help others, even if they don't really deserve that treatment, is usually what drives the victim back to their partner. If this isn't the case, most abusers also know just how to get their victims back where they want them.

A staple of abusive personalities is that the "best" and most manipulative abusers are incredibly charismatic. They understand precisely how to get to their victims and make them feel loved again. They might suddenly turn up in behavior, begin rewarding them with presents and genuine sentiment again. Most importantly, they'll credit this change to them. Assuring their victim that they've helped them be a better person reverses the feelings that the victim might have had prior. They go back to the abuser, thinking that things will be different now that the partner has started being better and more in control of their actions.

In reality, however, this is usually just a part of the abuser's plan. They know that they don't have to change, and they never plan to. They just know that they have to do this over and over for as long as they need until they have everything they wanted out of that victim. They'll keep acting out and trapping the victim in the cycle of abuse, then pulling them back in with a feigned change of heart just as they're about to quit on the relationship and leave.

It seems hard to believe that someone would fall for this same trick more than once—it's difficult for most people to give out chances beyond the second mistake. However, victims of abuse are connected to other victims of abuse. They feel compelled to stay with them and to make good on the love and attention that they never got to receive themselves.

In a way, the victim trying to care for their partner is the victim attempting to live vicariously through the people they try to help. The abuser of that victim, who has probably long given up on healing properly from their own experiences and trauma, understands this desire and is sure to take advantage of this at every turn. As time progresses, the victim feels more and more lost. They keep going back and forth between the hope that they can improve their own relationship and the crushing defeat when they go back only to visit that same conclusion—that they're going to be trapped in that relationship with someone who mistreats them.

This is the entire over-arching dilemma of an abusive relationship. When the abuser grows tired of the false kindness, they make all bad things feel as though they're the fault of the victim. The victim is used to having these feelings pushed on them, and they rarely learn how to really deal with that blame coming from other people, in addition to coming from their own internal narrative. They don't want to feel as though they're the root of all their relationship problems, but they also can't help but instill this own fear inside them.

Once you can get rid of this crushing fear inside you and shed the responsibility you feel over the wellbeing of other people, especially other people in your life who might not even care about you, you can learn to actively defend yourself against your abuser's emotional manipulation tactics. You can unlock the part of your life that you were meant to live—the part which is full of love and care, the part that was always waiting for you. This part of your life may have been held back from you by other people trying to pull you down, but you're the only one who can truly unlock it for yourself.

Chapter 6:
Secret Manipulation Tactics Abusers Don't Want You To Know

Abusers aren't unintelligent people—many of them are very smart, allowing them to understand how to manipulate you and how efficiently they can do so while keeping you around. However, the way that they keep you around is very simple. These tactics, at their core, are simply deflected and you can protect against them every single time if you're able to trust your gut and understand what you're looking for. In general, the tactics of an abuser are based around the emotions of the victim and the lack thereof on the part of the abuser. While this can seem very cruel on their part, they do understand the emotions of others to a literal extent. They don't understand their own emotions sometimes. They don't understand how the emotions of other people apply to them or how they can actually connect with people genuinely.

The main defense mechanism that a victim can use to their advantage is eliminating the element of surprise. This is what the abuser uses to rip the floor out from under their victim every single time they pull them back in with their charisma. In short, stop wondering what to expect—expect what to wonder. Being able to react quickly to potentially abusive and dangerous situations empowers you to act on them in a way you might not have been able to if you were stuck with no clue of what was happening around you. Being perceptive and becoming used to the tactics of your abuser can and will help you get out of that relationship. Abusers tend to follow some kind of pattern, and they fall back on these patterns more often than not. So look for those cycles of behaviors, track them, and a way to escape that abuse will become apparent.

In addition to understanding why the tactics work, you have to understand why they work on you in particular. More abusers pick their victims for a reason. Like I've said before, many abusers know how to pick out an empath or someone else who's suffered trauma in the past. Think about what part of your personality leaves you open to being taken advantage of. This doesn't mean that you should ever assume that the abuse is your own fault. But you should always be considering how you can be more careful of your own sake in the future. Being able to protect yourself not only from this abuse but from the possibility of abuse like this in the future keeps you safe and aware. Many victims fall into the "this will be different" mentality and allow their optimism to function over their sense of logic, pulling them back into the cycle of abuse with a different emotional manipulator. There are many tactics on this list that your abuser has never used because they just might not work on you so well. Others, you may know far too well for comfort—because that particular tactic is especially effective on you for whatever reason. As you read, put yourself in the shoes of the collective "you" and consider what those reasons might be.

The first tactic that abusers use might be the most

all-encompassing. All abusers will try to guilt you into feeling as though a bad relationship is your fault, even if there's no reasonable way this could be true. Simply put, this way of pushing **guilt and shame** onto the victim forces them into submission and makes them much more likely to stick around. The abuser makes up some narrative in which the fault truly lies with the victim and they should feel guilty. The victim often doesn't really have a way to stick up for themselves or argue back, so they simply take that blame.

For example, a date might go sour or the couple may fight for a long time one night. In reality, it might be that the abuser was at fault for the fight or whatever ruined the date. Or, there might have been no reason at all—just bad luck or a culmination of unfortunate circumstances. However, the abuser will try to make the victim feel as though it's their fault that these things happen, or that the victim could have prevented them. When this issue crops up in the middle of a fight or in your own relationship, take a step back and try to think your own way through the story. Don't automatically accept the way your partner sees it as the truth. Accept your own narrative before theirs.

Abusers will often try to **force an answer** or solution out of the victim when there isn't one. There may be a problem at work, with family, or in a relationship, and the two might be at a complete loss. The abuser, as I've mentioned before, can't stand not being in control of whatever's happening at any given moment, so they need to have an answer to whatever's in front of them. They'll often try to get this answer from their victim if they can't produce it on their own. They'll try to push you to answer something or give a solution to a problem you just can't solve. They know that the problem isn't something you have the knowledge, time, energy, etc. to solve, but they keep pushing it on you regardless.

This works on many victims because it pushes them out of their comfort zone and puts them off balance.

It can catch them off guard to be asked something like this by their significant other, and they want to help. However, they also know that they really can't, but they try anyway and end up just hurting themselves or disappointing their partner. This reinforces the shame and a feeling of worthlessness we were talking about. As a victim, be able to say no to requests that make you uncomfortable. Be able to calmly deny requests you can't fulfill.

Most abusers are relatively petty in the way that they interact with their victims once they're upset. When they're in this upset state, they involve someone else to do the communicating for them. Hence they are cutting themselves off from the victim and reinforcing the feeling that whatever the miscommunication was originally about is the victim's fault. This is called **triangulation**—someone else is brought into a fight between a couple and communicates for one side as a third party.

Think back to a fight you might have had with your significant other, and they had a friend "talk" for a period of time thereon. This is an example of triangulation, and it works on most victims because it makes them feel cut off from their partner. When the abuser refuses to speak to their victim and work things out in a normal and healthy way, the victim is made to feel more alone than they did previously. It can be very difficult to work through that feeling and actually understand when something is the abuser's fault, and it usually takes some practice. If you see your partner trying to use a third party to communicate with you, refuse to indulge them. Only agree to speak to your partner—it isn't anybody else's business what you were fighting about, and your partner needs to understand that.

Your abuser loves to play the **victim card** whenever they see the chance. This is the underlying root of a lot of different **manipulation tactics**. The classic abuser knows how to take advantage of almost every situation and turn it on its head so that you look like the bad guy. If they can make it seem not only to other people, but to you, that you're somehow an antagonist or even abusive yourself, they win over you. Imagine you're having some kind of fight, and your partner just stops and begins firing back at you with everything you've ever done wrong to them. Every time you fought back against them; they can spin it into you starting the fight. Every time you look for help outside of them, they can spin it as betraying them or even being promiscuous.

They know how to get inside your head and under your skin, and how they can mess with your perception of yourself and the relationship. Understand that you cannot ever accept their narrative before your own. Ask other people who you trust and who support you about anything that's been going on and listen to the way they see things. Getting other people's opinions can help you form a more clear-headed narrative of the relationship, and you can get the power dynamic back.

When you feel like you're teetering on the edge of finally deciding to leave your abuser and abandon the relationship for your own sake, your abuser might try to pull you back in with their **love-bombing** tactics.

Love-bombing, a tactic I've touched on before in which the abuser will almost harass you with praise and love and shows of affection until you start to become infatuated with them again. The way that an abuser will love-bomb you varies from person to person, but most of them will either be very showy, or very gentle. Showy love-bombing includes things like public displays of affection and loudly declaring feelings for you.

This implements social obligation on top of the obligation you might feel toward them individually. You feel more compelled to accept and forgive when you're surrounded by onlookers. More gentle love-bombing establishes the decaying sense of connection and intimacy between the two of you—

genuine sentiment and handholding are signs of gentle love-bombing. They're meant to get you back on their side and flood your system with the dopamine you experienced when you first met them so that you feel the relationship is able to be salvaged.

As a victim, be careful when your abuser suddenly starts to get incredibly nice to you seemingly out of nowhere. Be aware that there can be plenty of reasons for the sudden change of heart, some of them malicious.

In addition to playing the victim, you abuser will often try to get some kind of **pity** out of you. When you fight or almost separate, they'll do everything they can to remind you of the fact that they've also endured abuse, just like you. They'll do everything in their power to make themselves look like someone broken and hurt, just another victim of the cruel world around them. They know this works because they know just how empathetic you are, just how willing you are to backtrack and risk your own happiness for them. They know that and they're more than willing to take advantage of that.

They handpicked you because of your kindness, your ability to connect with others in a much more intimate and personal way. Because they know how much you can connect with them, especially as another victim of trauma, they also know they can get a lot of pity out of you. They know that you'll see them as someone broken, someone who needs help just like you do, and they know you'll try to help them, even if it means staying with them and being knowingly unhappy. If you see your abuser start to retract and they seem to become sadder or moping around you, keep this in mind—everything they do is to manipulate your feelings. Be wary of every emotion they express in your presence.

On the flip side of your abuser's emotional spectrum, they might notice that the softer side of their feelings isn't quite working on you. So, they might try to simply intimidate you into agreeing with them or staying with them. They know that they have to keep you at their side at all costs, so they'll limit where you can go and when, with whom, for how long. They have the means to limit these things and they'll know where you are. The obsessive traits of the abuser know no bounds, and they'll usually have some way to track you and know where you are so they can monitor your behavior and who you're hanging around.

This **intimidation** usually comes in the wake of pity of some wave of sadness that they had expressed near you. They might notice that you aren't paying as much attention to them and their antics, so they'll switch their emotions to make you more afraid to resist or run away. They'll hide this intimidation behind an act of "love," or they'll claim to just want to keep you as safe as possible. If you see this happening, don't let your abuser bully you into a belief. Understand that you have to keep yourself safe but maintain your belief and know that you are the victim of their abuse, not the other way around. This intimidation is not love, it's harassment.

To go right along with these methods of intimidation, many abusers will plainly bully and harass their victims into submission. They understand what makes their victims afraid of them and why they're afraid of other people—they understand much about their victim and use all the intimate understanding they have of them to their advantage. This includes not only the kind of intimidation that presents itself more discreetly but also plain bullying and verbal harassment. This is where intimidation really becomes abuse for the victim, and they're driven into a place where they feel forced to submit. The key thing about this particular method of abuse and manipulation is that the victim might feel as though they have to fight back, that they have to stand up for themselves of the abuse will only become worse.

In reality, the situation is usually made worse when the victim tries to fight back. As a victim undergoing this abusive treatment, you must understand that there are ways to resist your abuser and fight back that don't necessarily involve physically fighting with them. Don't make it obvious—your resistance to their manipulation should be quiet and discreet. This way, you have a better chance of getting out without them noticing. Your priority should be your own safety, and that means you have to lay low on their radar from time to time.

As petty as most abusers are, it's the simplest and most petty methods of bullying that can get to you the most easily. Many abusers simply revert to being accusatory, calling their partner names and trying to demean them, making them feel as small and defenseless as possible. This **name-calling** might start off slow and small—during a fight, your abuser might suddenly call you a name or use a phrase that they know really affects you. They apologize, and you forgive them. But it keeps happening more and more as time goes on. Every fight you have, they call you named and verbally abuse you with nicknames and terms that make your blood boil. They're trying to get a rise out of you.

If you do react verbally to them, they know how they can get you off balance and surprise you. If they know how to rile you up, they also know how to force you into submission. This is just another way that the abuser tries to shift the power balance and keep it on their side for as long as possible. As a victim who might be watching this unfold between you and your partner right now, make sure that you can control your feelings; don't let them get an emotional reaction out of you. Remove yourself from the fight if you can, but don't let your abuser see you break down.

On the complete opposite side of the abuser's emotional spectrum again, they might completely shut down as soon as you leave a fight or get riled up towards them. They see this as a way of punishing you. And it especially works if you are incredibly attached to their partner.

Shutting off someone who thrives on verbal communication from being able to talk to their partner can really do a number of their confidence, and it can make them feel intensely alone. This isolating feeling is usually enough, after a period of time, to get the victim to forgive the abuser for whatever happened. At that point, the punishment has served its course, and the abuser feels dominant once again over the victim. This manipulation tactic is a game of emotional stamina. The victim will never win because the abuser has less of an attachment to the victim than the other way around.

If you're someone on the receiving end of this silent treatment, understand that it's ok for you to feel alone and to want to talk to them again. Try not to let them win, but if you have to, just know that you shouldn't have to. If you take that loss, keep your head up and keep a level head.

Rules and restrictions are a massive part of the

dynamics between an abuser and the victim of that person's abuse. The abuser manipulates what the victim can do and when, for how long, and why, so that the victim becomes used to that feeling of being submissive to their partner. However, the rules and restrictions within that relationship aren't always enforced. **Intermittent reinforcement** is a way for the abuser to keep the victim confused on how to please their partner. Say you did something that the abuser usually likes, and they reward you with praise. You understand the praise and make the connection between the action and the positive result. However, consider a few months later when you do that same thing again but receive no reward, or even your partner becomes angry with you over the action. Even though you expected a positive result, your partner intentionally upset that cause and effect by giving a neutral or negative reaction to the same thing you did.

This different reaction disconnects the action from the effect, leaving you wondering what you did wrong and how you can fix it. This gets the victim in the habit of always trying to help and serve their partner. As a victim, don't dote too much on a strange reaction. If need be, just ask them straightforwardly what was different. Make changes if you feel the need to, but only then.

After you've spent a while with your abuser, you might notice a shift in the way they treat your issues and reactions versus the way they expect their own to be treated. If you have a problem or you react emotionally to something, your abuser might try to "calm you down" by assuring you that you're simply **overreacting**. They'll spin your reaction to seem bigger than it was or make it out to be a less proportionate reaction to the actual problem. They might try and assure you that the problem isn't actually a problem, or that you're just making a big deal out of nothing. By comparison, they'll treat only their own problems and outbursts as the top priority, and they expect you to consider them your own top priority as well.

This is the abuser's way of making sure you consider their problems before your own. And it also reinforces the idea that the victim should rely more on the abuser's narrative of what happened before their own, messing up their perception of reality. Again, you should never ever take the way your abuser spins situations as the reality—there is always something they're blowing out of proportion or minimizing to make their own issues look more important. Remember to take care of yourself before anyone else, and always make sure that your health is your own first priority.

The classic abuser will always try to lie to you at every turn. They take every single opportunity they can get by lying to you, cheating you out of your own feelings, making you feel small, and messing up the way you understand reality and the way things actually play out around you. One of the most frequent ways that your abuser might lie to you is through **omission**.

Lies of omission are not technically lies, but they are a way for your partner to intentionally keep the truth from you or pit you against a friend or family member. This is a way they can keep you away from other people or get you to rely on them and the way they recount events instead of your own narrative. If your partner tells you something that happened, you would be inclined to naturally believe them. You might get into a fight with a friend or a loved one and your partner might become your way of interacting with them. Your partner might intentionally keep information from you and prevent you from interacting with that loved one, therefore also preventing you from being able to rely on that loved one and become close with them again. If you can, try to avoid having to rely on your abuser for information and make sure you have a way to fact-check everything they say.

The lies of the abuser culminate in one of the most influential and damaging manipulation tactics that you, as a victim, can deal with. **Gaslighting** occurs when an abuser makes their partner question the way they're interpreting events and wonder if the narrative they're building of the reality around them is actually real. When you and your abuser fight over something, the abuser may try to minimize your reactions and assure you that the way you're getting upset isn't appropriate, because what you're getting upset over didn't actually happen the way you think it did. Insisting that you're incorrect about things you saw or heard, over a long period of time, becomes incredibly damaging to the victim. They start to question not only their eyes and their perception but their sanity at its core. They start to wonder why they see things the way they do if there's something wrong with them and their own perception. The abuser does this intentionally to get the victim to rely on them more and to get them used to deferring to them.

That deference gives them the power to build whatever narrative they really want. As a victim, observe what parts of the story your abuser always seems to disagree with. Do whatever you can to get a second opinion from someone else and never trust your abuser's story until you can check it with a neutral party who knows what really happened.

When you finally decide to confront your abuser and ask about something, or you even just ask a question they don't have the kind of answer they need to, they'll evade the question. Abusers spend most of their time evading questions and trying to distract you from what's really going on in the relationship. They'll do anything they can to distract you from reality—they might distract you from the dark parts of their manipulative behavior by trying to suddenly be overly kind to you. Or, on the other hand, they often try to deflect the blame from themselves onto you, instead insinuating that you shouldn't be asking them the question in the first place.

The abuser will often play the victim here, trying to gain your pity and reverting back to the state of someone overcome with trauma and who needs help. They play up this broken act until you finally drop the question and you again shift back to wanting to care for them. They can't allow you to dig too deep or find a weak spot in the narrative they're building. If you're a victim going through this cycle of diversion and evasion, make sure you stay on topic. Don't let yourself be swayed by a rapid change of subject, and don't give in to their emotional manipulation. They can wait until you have your answer to throw a pity party.

Often, abusers will switch back and forth between **hot and cold**, so to speak. At one point, they may give you the cold shoulder and ignore you at every turn. At some other points in the relationship, they might react violently or aggressively to very small arguments of disagreements over minute things. They do this to keep the victim from being able to settle into a comfortable pattern of thinking. Much like the intermittent reinforcement, the hot and cold back and forth for the abuser is just a way to make sure the victim doesn't get too comfortable associating a certain action with a positive or negative response. If they're constantly being caught off guard by different reactions that might be contradictory to reactions in the past, the victim has no secure logic to go off of when it comes to their partner's reactions. Make sure that you have someone else around you who's more stable in your life and who you can rely on. Don't pay any more attention to your abuser's outbursts than you have to.

Similar to their habit of simply leaving out important information, many abusers will also seem to develop a habit of **willingly forgetting things** that happen that make them look bad. However, they'll very rarely let go of things that have happened that make you look bad instead of them.

This is just another way that your abuser will try to pin you down and make you believe that you're a bad person or that you don't deserve to be feeling the way that you do. The reason that these tactics work so well is that the victim is probably already relatively used to feeling as though they aren't allowed to feel the way they do, or like they have no right to be upset over something. Someone who has been a victim of abuse in the past might have a hard time letting go of their bad habits and negative ways of thinking from their past abusers.

The current manipulator knows this and takes advantage of the way that many victims already have a tendency to blame themselves sometimes. As a victim, know that this is wrong, that this is abuse. Always keep a record to yourself of what happened and when. If you need to, keeping a physical diary of your abuse can help be a comfort when you question if what you experienced was real and valid. Know that toxic relationships very often rely on making you feel crazy and that anything your abuser tries to tell you isn't necessarily true or relevant.

Even if you can confront your abuser and try to get them to understand that something happened exactly the way you thought it did, that doesn't mean that you've suddenly gotten through to that abuser. They'll still find a way to either completely avoid the blame or spin the blame onto you.

This is how the abuser operates—they physically **can't take the responsibility** for anything, even if it's very obviously their fault. This is the main flaw in the charming and charismatic abuser; they can't own up to anything, even something that is of no detriment to them or something that happened years ago. They're narcissistic, and they find it incredibly difficult to believe that anything that's ever happened was genuinely their fault. They especially won't accept this assertion from someone they look down on and regularly abuse.

This deflection of blame is actually usually more about their own flaws than it is about cornering and blaming their victim instead. But this blame is usually a byproduct of their inability to take the blame for anything. As a victim, put yourself first and distance yourself from the abuser is you feel the need to. Your safety and health are both more important than the comfort of your abuser, and you need to be able to properly prioritize yourself.

Understand that your abuser acting out and generally being childish are both not your fault—no way that they treat you is ever your fault.

Hypnosis might not be something you think of when you consider the way that you might be a victim of abuse. But trance can play a fairly large role when it comes to how your abuser affects you and what they do to you, how they alter the way you think and to what extent. We all go into some state of trance at some point in our lives, whether it be when we're driving down the road or really intensely focused on our favorite book.

Trance is a heightened state of focus, but it's also a state in which we have a lack of focus on the things going on around us. Abusers have a similar effect on their victims sometimes, make it so that the victim can't help but only focus on their relationship with the abuser while their other relationships fade out of that focus. That lets the abuser truly cut the victim off from the outside world and take advantage of them to the fullest of their desires.

Don't let the abuser give you this sense of tunnel vision! If you let yourself only focus on the abuser, you let them win. Make sure you keep in touch with people outside the relationship and do your best to keep those relationships alive and well. You may need to rely on them in the future, so make sure your awareness isn't completely limited to the abuser. The person right in front of you isn't ever the only one that matters.

When the abuser fights you on the way things happen, it won't always be in a way that makes it obvious that they're actually trying to fight you on it. They're trying to win the argument, and they're also trying to break you down and make you question your sanity. To do this, they'll phrase their denial in a patronizing, **passive-aggressive way**. Their goal at this point is just to make sure you aren't sure of yourself or your perception. You may be fighting over something with them, and they'll refute your claims in a more passive way. Where they might have otherwise simply told you that you were wrong before presenting their "side" of the story, they'll now accuse you of other things alongside their accusation of your false understanding. Instead of saying "no, it happened this way," they'll begin to ask, "are you sure that's what happened?" They ask this way to make it seem like they're trying to help you or give you the benefit of the doubt so that they don't seem too combative.

In reality, they know you're already questioning yourself a lot, and they intend to capitalize on that unsure nature. Make sure you can keep an actual documentation of what actually happened. Or at least have someone you can talk to who has a neutral understanding of the events and can present them in an unbiased way. The abuser just wants to upset you before pulling you back in and making it seem like they're a good person.

This façade, this trick that spells out that they're actually a good—or at least a broken and helpless person, is the most dangerous one you'll encounter during your time with the abuser. They'll push you away and abuse and drive you insane but draw you right back in as soon as you start to pull away from their own volition. They know what you want out of them and they're more than willing to dangle it right in front of you until they know they can do whatever they want with you. They know exactly how to appeal to your desire to help them, your desire to help anyone you meet who's gone through something similar to you.

In the infinite cruelty of the manipulative abuser, they understand your despair and the things you've been through and they know how much you want to help them. Although they don't want the pity of your real aid, they do want to keep you in their life so they can keep preying on you. This is what you really have to realize while in an abusive relationship. Your abuser does not care about you, does not care about your feelings, and does not want your help. This is hurtful to finally realize but understanding it and taking control of that fact will help you get out of a terrible relationship. Even though your abuser doesn't want your help, you can still help yourself.

Chapter 7:
What To Do When You Can't Just Run Away

In an ideal world, every victim of abuse could get out of their abusive relationship and never see their abuser again. In an ideal world, it really could be that easy. The victim could finally stand up for themselves and say no, file a restraining order if need be, and run away to never see their manipulator again.

Unfortunately, we don't live in that world. Many victims can run away from their abusers and live with friends and family until they can get back on their feet. Many victims can live out that ideal where they stand their ground and never have to see the person who ruined a part of their life again. Unfortunately, this isn't the case for many other victims of abuse. In many cases, the victim is never given the opportunity to run away when they need to.

As tempting as it can be, it's never a good idea to start fighting back suddenly against your manipulator. Although they may be abusing you verbally or emotionally and not physically, that can be subject to change if they feel the need to keep you submissive more forcefully. Things can get very violent very quickly if you start verbally or physically fighting back, and you need to consider your own health and safety before you consider your ability to leave the relationship.

When you do decide that you need to stop just taking the abuse, make sure you have the people you need to turn to. These people can be your family, your friends, a group of colleagues, as long as they're people you can trust and who make you feel safe and comfortable. This group of people will come to be your support system for the foreseeable future while you figure out a way to deal with your partner.

The support system can serve a variety of purposes.

As you come to terms with your abuse and begin figuring out ways you can deal with it without jeopardizing yourself and your safety, you should be able to go to this group of loved ones for safety and refuge. Don't suddenly begin relying on them constantly, however, or else your partner may notice and become suspicious that you're trying to leave them. Treat them like any other normal group of friends—ideally, you should be able to spend at least some time with them where you can vent and express your frustrations.

Having a support group can also help to reestablish what it's like to have normal social interactions. Usually, victims of a long abusive relationship become detached from their other social circles, so they can forget what it's like to have friends and family who they can interact with normally without fear. This is what your support system is for— reintroducing the sensation of socializing normally without the fear of your partner or spouse looming over you. Regaining this ability to socialize normally is crucial when you begin rebuilding your life and will have to socialize with new people.

After a long period where you only interacted with mostly one socially abnormal person, just having a lunch date can be a foreign concept to the victim. Being able to rely on people around you who can get you more used to normal socialization without having to be afraid of people is a very useful skill. If you just spent time around your abuser, you'll eventually be pulled back into the cycle of abuse that you endured before you convinced yourself to leave.

This pull can be very strong, as the abuser is very charismatic. They want to make you believe that everything you're arguing against, everything you're fighting about is really your fault and your own overreactions. The more time you spend around them, the more they'll get you to really believe that for yourself as well. The more time you spend with your abuser, the more you start to believe that maybe you are going crazy and maybe you are being too emotional.

The most important thing to be able to maintain when you're trying to distance yourself from an abusive relationship in which you can't actually run away is your sense of self-worth. Being able to care for yourself when your abuser tries to make you believe you don't have that right is empowering and can refresh you when your abuser is wearing you down. Something as small or as simple as reading a book you enjoy, taking a silent bath, indulging in comfort food, or meditation can be really beneficial to your mental and emotional health.

This book isn't predominantly about abusers who target your physical wellbeing. No, the place the abusers described in this book will try to hurt you is in your confidence, your self-esteem, your emotional strength. The abuser wants to make you feel weak and as though you can't rely on yourself, so you're more likely to rely on them. This is their ultimate goal and they'll do anything to achieve it.

Once they know you only feel comfortable talking to them and relying emotionally on them, they have the confidence to do whatever they want with you, make you feel as low and as broken as they want. Over time, they damage you over and over and wear you down. Having a support system in place can effectively make sure you don't completely go insane while having to deal with this abuse. In addition to reintroducing normal social situations to you, having a support system also reconnects you to your sense of self and belonging.

Belonging to a group of friends and loved ones outside your abuser or their awareness can help you to heal emotionally and mentally. You need to have people around you who are different from your abuser, who can let you vent and who can allow you to rebuild your self-worth. If you have people in your life who let you be as flawed as you want and still accept you and love you, you can learn to accept yourself as a flawed human as well. Abusers instill this weird perception in our head where we think we have to be perfect; we have to please others, we have to do everything we can to hide away everything imperfect about ourselves.

Having a proper support system can help get rid of this unhealthy understanding of ourselves and just take ourselves as flawed humans. There's nothing wrong with having flaws and there's especially nothing wrong with having problems accepting them. People who love you will take you as you are—and you'll be able to rediscover what it feels like to be really, genuinely loved. We so often forget how being loved and cared about feels and having people in our lives who replace the abuse of our toxic partner with genuine love and affection offsets the hurt that the partner does to us and our hearts. Being introduced to people who love you and expect nothing in return is very new for people who are used to just being abused. So it can take a lot of time for the victim to heal through these people and this new love.

Unfortunately, we're not always able to escape our

abusers for our loved ones and our support system. There will come times where the victim has to deal with their abuser with no way to get away from the emotional manipulation. The abuser might be constantly trying to manipulate the way you think things happen and to break you down. If you want to have a way to record the reality without being able to contact a third party, keep a journal of events that happen to you. When you can keep a physical journal of the things that have happened to you and you're able to make note of them immediately when they happen or almost directly after, you can build your own reliable narrative which you can cling to once your abuser tries to dismantle your sense of reality. This physical way to take note of the world around you can be written, like a normal journal or diary. Or, you can record videos of yourself to keep note of the abuse over months or years. Having this record of how you felt and why, hearing it from yourself, can help you stay in touch and remember that you're the victim in the relationship—the abuser will try to persuade you to the idea that you're overreacting and that you aren't really as much of a victim as you think.

Be aware of how your abuser's behavior changes. In addition to keeping a record of your own feelings, keep a record of your abuser as well. Being able to see patterns in their behavior and what they might correlate to will help you navigate the abuse better. If you can do what they like and what makes them happier with minimal abuse to yourself and your mental state, that's the idea—being able to navigate the often confusing emotions of your abuser will help you to be healthier and happier in the relationship, as well as avoid them and their negative mood swings as much as you can without actually being able to leave that relationship.

It's often very difficult to navigate an abuser who does their best to throw you off your balance—they do everything in their power to make their emotions seem more confusing than they actually are, and that makes actually learning their patterns that much more rewarding. If you can find a way to keep track of how they react to certain things, you can figure out how to get them in a certain mood. In a way, this perfectly allows you to manipulate your abuser right back, giving them a taste of their own medicine.

Take the time out of your day to care for yourself when you don't have a support system immediately at your disposal. If you do, you should always try to use it, but learn to rely on yourself for that support every once in a while, too. The abuser tries to keep the power dynamic in their favor by getting you to need them and rely on them for every little thing. If you can wrench even that small control over your life from their hands and care for yourself, you've won that small battle. Those small battles pile up over time and become the most important aspect of getting out of your abusive relationship. Being able to become independent isn't just soft words and self-care, though; caring for yourself includes things you don't want to do. Responsibilities, paying bills, taking care of the home of your own accord instead of whenever somebody asks you to; these are all things that you should be able to do on your own without support from other people. It's difficult to get that ball rolling if you've been relying on your abuser for long enough, but the payoff of that action makes the tireless hours of chores and management more than worth it.

After you've become more independent, you have the power to manage yourself without any help from anyone, including your abuser. While it is important to rely on your supporters, it's perhaps even more important that you don't need them all the time.

The point of becoming independent and having this support system is not at all to just bide your time—you're making these preparations for yourself because you're soon going to be able to finally get out of the relationship that's been holding you back for months, even years. The path to getting up and becoming dependent, empowered, and back to a normal emotional space is rocky and not linear. There are days where you feel that you're ready and days that you feel you never will be ready. All of these come with the ebb and flow of our emotions. We'll never always feel ready, but there will come a day when you have to be ready, to leave your abuser once and for all.

As we'll go over in the next and final chapter, the hardest part about separating from your abuser is not the actual act of letting go and leaving them in the moment. The short term is the easiest part. The difficulty comes after weeks and months of being away from them. Abuse of all kinds, as I've said before, is much like an addiction. It eats away at you slowly but surely, and you have to find your own way out of it. It's easy to declare that you'll never indulge in your addiction again. It's easy to go a day or two without it. However, your brain becomes used to this thing that gave it dopamine, gave it happiness and elation. Because your brain is so used to that sensation, they need it and they crave it for weeks, months on end. You feel the need to go back to your addiction, just one more, one more shot or one more chance or just a little more so you can really feel as though you're finally done. You're tricking yourself, and your brain is tricking you when you do this. Going back to your abuser is just like going back to an addiction you swore you had conquered—it happens to many victims, sometimes more than once.

Even after the push and pull when we finally leave, we feel as though we're leaving an important part of ourselves behind. As a victim, you have to make peace with the part of yourself that you'll leave with that relationship. Even if you can't get that part of you back, you don't need to.

Humans of all kinds are made to grow and change and develop. They're supposed to always be adapting to new environments and new people and new ways to overcome obstacles. We develop a new part of us, similarly, when we encounter new and different environments. Those new environments might be a new home, a new job, or a new relationship. When you find a new environment, you must leave the old one behind.

In this sense, you have to leave the sense of obligation you feel toward the abuser with them, with that relationship. Understand that your abuser has made you feel this way and understand that you shouldn't ever be ok with that. You can't save everyone, all the time. There are people who you can help, who will listen to you and let you aid them. Abusers simply turn a blind eye to the help they might know they need. They understand that they need some form of emotional or psychological help, but their own wellbeing isn't often on their mind. What is on their mind, plain and simple, is their need for control—their need to at least feel as though they're in control. You need to be the person who moves on from them, the one to help yourself. There are many people who you can help in your lifetime, but there is only one person you can ever really save—yourself.

Chapter 8:
What's Next?
First Aid Advice To Get Through The Day And Gain Freedom Over The Long Run

At some point or another, you will be presented with the opportunity to finally leave your abuser once and for all. This is a process that's exciting, and so you might feel the urge to get it over and done with as fast as you can. However, up and leaving your abuser with absolutely no build-up to it can lead to complications and can cause your partner to act out and potentially become more violent or aggressive than they needed to be.

Before you leave them, make sure they understand that you know exactly what they're doing and that it isn't going to work on you. Drop subtle hints to them over time and make sure they get a general understanding of your current emotional state. Don't react so much to their pity parties and hold yourself a little higher. When you were building up your confidence in preparation for leaving your abuser, it was wise to make sure you still kept your head down and your eyes averted so that your abuser wouldn't catch on.

Now that you're in a place where you can actually leave your abuser and be ok financially and emotionally, there's no harm in making sure they know that you're feeling better, that you're not dependent on them anymore, and that you don't need them and won't need them ever again.

Of course, don't make these hints so over the top that your abuser may become angry, but make sure that it's enough to clue them in to the fact that you'll be leaving them. Drop ideas of separation to them and get into small disputes with them over things that you're confident won't result in an escalation. This way, you make yourself seem more distant and much less reliable as a victim. The abuser will see you as less desirable and may separate from you on their own terms.

However, many abusers are too stubborn to give up on your or their control over you, so don't count on your petty squabbles to be enough to get them to let you go on their own.

When you're really ready to leave them once and for all, make sure you still have your support system in place—the loved ones who are around you and who will support you through this time will be absolutely priceless. Even if you know you're ready to leave them, understand that separating from a toxic partner is still stressful.

The entire situation and process is extremely taxing on you emotionally. It's a good thing to have people close to you who you can rely on and fall back on just in case you suddenly need that support. By now, you should be able to be more self-reliant and able to take care of most things by yourself. And this will be much easier once you're away from the partner for enough time—but that doesn't mean you won't have moments of weakness or vulnerability.

It's during these moments that you should have good people around you so that you can learn to properly trust again, or at least get back on that path of normal and healthy relationships.

Unfortunately, most victims will need more than their support group in the long run when it comes to fully healing and regaining the person they once were before they entered that toxic relationship. If you're able to, it's always a good idea to consult a medical professional who has experience in the field of mental and emotional help. You might not find the person who suits you best when you look for this professional help, so bounce around and test the waters to see what works for you. Judge them by your own personal preferences and experiences but listen to what the professional has to say.

You need somebody outside your friend circle and/or someone who isn't a close loved one to confirm your feelings, validate your reactions to things, and point you toward the right goals for the future. While you should always trust the people in your support circle, the people who you trust will always be biased. Even a positive bias towards you can be damaging in the long run when they try to eliminate any blame on your end. As much as you should never try to blame yourself when it comes to the abuse you endured for that portion of your life, it also isn't healthy to think of yourself as someone who did nothing wrong throughout the entirety of the relationship.

Even though you entered the relationship likely because you were a kind and caring person, you were picked out by the abuser because you weren't wary of them. This is no sin but being gullible or kind to a fault can and will get you in a lot of negative situations in the future. Regardless, talking to a medical professional who you can trust is very important in addition to having a support system full of people who care for you. A medical professional knows what they're talking about and they have no bias towards you. Their agenda is completely neutral, so they have no plans to push any of their personal feelings onto you. They're trained not to project themselves onto you—unlike your loved ones—and they best know how to advise you when it comes to avoiding feelings over your abuser and simply moving farther away from them and heal as time goes on.

When your friend or loved one might tell you to get revenge or act on your emotions for the cathartic result, the therapist or professional knows how to best help you out of the negative emotions that can come immediately after separating from an abusive partner or spouse. They know what to advise against, and they know what can hurt you in the months following. Taking the advice of our friends and family is good and beneficial to you, but it's also very important to listen to people who actually know what they're talking about and how to help you the best from an objective standpoint.

You don't necessarily have to adopt this more objective approach if you don't want to—it may be better for you to feel the emotions you haven't been allowed for so long. It's cathartic to catch up and reconnect with your own feelings, but don't let them consume you. Acting on impulse can make you do something you might regret or worse; it could even drive you back to your abuser.

It's usually best for the victim of past abuse to put as much distance as they can between themselves and their ex. That distance can be very literal, and you may even file a restraining order against them if you need the extra assurance that they're less likely to bother you again. That distance should, at the very least, represent emotional distance.

Don't go out of the way to try to reconcile with your abuser after you've left them. Every single interaction you have with them after you initially leave, to them, is just a way that they can break down your defenses and get you back for them to keep abusing you. If you do end up getting back into touch with them, they'll do everything they can to convince you of one of two things. They'll either try to make you believe that this entire ordeal was actually your fault, and they'll try to guilt you into getting back with them out of shame. Or, on the other hand, they may beg and plead with you, acknowledging their wrongs and promising to make good on them if you just give them another chance. This can be very convincing, especially for victims who want to believe that they really can help their past abusers.

The abuser understands that their abuse is wrong, and many are more than willing to recognize it if they really feel the need to. Once they do, it might seem like they're trying to apologize and really try again. Don't fall for this trick more than you might have already while you were actually in the relationship. As hard as it might be, you have to turn your back on the abuser. Even if you do think that their apology might be genuine, understand that you don't have to accept it regardless. Your abuser is not entitled to your pity or to your forgiveness, no matter their sincerity.

This hero complex that may have been driving you before to get back together with your ex or even forgive them at all, has to fall away in some regard before you can heal. Not only do you have to learn to let go of the part of yourself from that relationship. You also have to learn to let go of the feelings you developed during that time—that is to say, the unhealthy coping mechanisms that you might have used in order to ease the pain of that relationship. One of these coping mechanisms is usually trying to apologize for the abuser or making them seem more a victim than a perpetrator.

If you're an empath or just someone especially kind or empathetic for others, you feel the natural urge to defend the abuser, even though you fully know how much they hurt you over the time you were together. In order to let go of these feelings of defense for them, it might be better to discuss with either a professional or with your support system. Ask them what they thought of the abuser, or how they feel about defending them. Know that these people who consult are merely a second opinion, but you have to make the final decision to dismiss the feelings that might be negatively affecting you or warping your feelings about the abuser. Consider what they did to you that might have made you feel defensive of them. How did they speak to you during the relationship that might've made you uncomfortable? How often did certain arguments come up that made you feel guilty for that argument? Abusers so often employ ways of speaking and arguing that make you feel guilty for saying anything antagonistic, blaming them, or treating them like an equally guilty party to you. They want you to feel guilty for even giving the impression that you fault them for anything.

The most important thing is control, so knowing that you view them as a person who's broken, someone who needs help or assistance from you, someone who is only a victim of other sources of abuse and nothing more.

Everyone endures some kind of abuse at some point

in their life—we all do and we all will. This, of course, includes most abusers. Though they manipulate others, they all have something that pulls them down mentally. They have that abuse that they can bond with you over, something they force a bond with you over. Empaths are most willing to accept and return this bond, as they're usually desperate for some kind of relationship or camaraderie, even if it hurts them. They reciprocate the relationship because they need to with somebody, for that body to be with them and bond with anything over. The abuser takes advantage of how willing you are to bond with them, and they do anything to maintain it.

You have to let go of your sympathy for the abuser, let go of any pity you felt toward them, and learn that you can't fix the abuser even if you tried. The only person who could ever transform an abuser into someone healthy and functional is themselves. This result is unlikely, as abusers are usually fairly narcissistic and don't recognize when they need help or when they're doing something generally considered morally wrong.

They don't care about morals, a construct which they doubt will actually cause them success directly. Instead, they rely on this manipulation to propel them forward. It would be counterproductive as far as recovery goes to even attempt to fix the abuser before or after getting physically away from them.

Your life should effectively restart after you get away from them--consider yourself a blank slate for you to begin once again, as a new and clean person unaffected by your past experiences. Here are just a few of the ways you can clean that slate of yours and start again while reducing the probability of running into your abuser again or finding yourself drawn to them again once you're apart.

Properly assess your strengths and weaknesses— take a look at yourself from an outside perspective and consider your strengths and weaknesses. These are things you can improve upon in the future but just look at them as measurements or extensions of yourself physically. You may have a weak constitution, an excessive compulsion to try to help others, you may be too stubborn for your own good, or a massive amount of any other flaws in your personality.

Understanding yourself not just as a victim, but as an entire individual independent of your abuse can help you distance yourself from that abuse. Your identity as a human who exists outside the abuse you endure. Even when we leave an abusive or toxic relationship, we find ourselves connecting our personhood to that person or the relationship we recently left. Think of yourself not as a victim or the product of abuse, but as a human who is living their life. Your life is larger than any abuse you suffer, so conduct yourself as such.

Develop the ability to properly set boundaries— learn to say no. This is a lesson you were never able to properly learn or put in place while you were in the toxic relationship but make up for lost time by setting boundaries with the people around you. Don't see these boundaries as being made of fear or hate, or even uncertainty. You don't create boundaries healthily for the sake of keeping people away from you—this promotes a mindset in which you consider the world around you with fear and unease. Instead, think of these boundaries you set as an act of love for yourself, rather than fear of others. Understand that the boundaries you put in place are ultimately for the benefit of you and your mental health—they're to make sure you feel safe and secure.

Additionally, be sure that you set the boundaries you're most comfortable with. It's usually a good idea to ask a professional what some good boundaries are for your situation, but you're ultimately the one who must put them in place. Be sure that you don't accidentally get too close to you or do things you actually aren't ok with. Also, boundaries will change as you grow and come to understand yourself better after the relationship ends. The boundaries you set should grow alongside you, so don't be afraid to let your loved ones know when something changes. You may become more comfortable with a certain action or kind of contact, or you may realize you're less comfortable with something than you first thought. The importance is your comfort, so your boundaries should be an expression of self-love.

Stand your ground and stand up for yourself when you need to—as a continuation of setting your boundaries, be prepared for conflict based on those boundaries, or on other things. You will run into people who don't accept you as well as your support system does, and they may try to push you around or force things on you. This is something that will happen over time lots, so it's always good to practice rebuilding your confidence and ability to defend yourself which deteriorated while you were in an abusive relationship.

Keep in mind that the first priority should always be

you—maybe not for the group, but just for you and from your perspective. Your top priority should always be defending your beliefs, at least when you first begin standing up for yourself and practicing standing your ground. You don't need to be aggressive or fight back against the person disagreeing with you, but you should be able to assert yourself and state your reasons calmly, but confidently.

There will be times where you receive backlash for leaving your abuser—it can be dangerous for some people regardless of whether they leave their abuser or stay with them. So they choose the lesser of two evils and escape to their loved ones. The abuser may try to get back into touch with you, contacting you however they can at first. After that, they might even try to physically see you and confront you personally. This can be risky, so don't be ashamed if you need to hide from them until you can get the situation under control. This might mean either waiting out the storm or seeking legal action, like a restraining order.

Being emotionally ready for the backlash can be much more difficult than being prepared for it emotionally, so prepare yourself in the mental sense for the things that might happen after you forcibly exit the relationship. Make sure your support system is made up of people that can and will help to hide you from your abuser and make sure you have places you could go other than your support system if they couldn't hide you. This could mean contacting authorities or making sure you know where the nearest/cheapest hotel is in the case of an emergency. The most important thing is your safety, so understand how you can best defend yourself when worse comes to worst.

There might be some cases where you can't escape the abuse because of your relation to them, where they're family or somebody you're obligated to see from time to time. If this is the case, do everything you can to avoid contact with them and reduce the amount you have to interact with them.

In addition, develop an exit plan for when you do have to be with them. Planning and having contingency plans can be a great method of keeping you at ease in times where you have to be around your abuser in public or in private. So spend some time on your own considering what you would most likely do in any situation where you would need to get out of there. Have a pack ready with a small amount of supplies, including water and a small amount of food. Have a general idea of where you would go upon certain contingencies and think about what your next moves would be after you were forced to leave.

My next book will be about how to actually defend yourself against the attacks of the emotional abuser. It will deal with the action that goes on between you and the abuser leading up to you having to leave them. It's very important that, in addition to understanding your own worth, you also understand how to best defend yourself actively against the tactics of an abuser and how to fight back against them without putting yourself in any potential danger.

After all, this is what this book has been about—how to keep yourself out of danger whenever possible. While my next book will dive more into the active nature of defending yourself against emotional and psychological abuse, it's most important that you can guarantee your own safety. If you can't do that, you should try to fight back against your abuser. Although it seems more justified to fight back against them whenever you can, fighting back directly can result in the abuse becoming physical. This is the last thing we want to happen, so do yourself a favor and keep yourself as safe as you can.

Conclusion

This book is not meant to prevent any harm from befalling you. Abuse is scary and the people behind it are unpredictable. It can be terrifying to try to deal with abusers head-on, and you are incredibly brave for doing so. If nothing else, appreciate yourself and your bravery already for being able to keep calm in the midst of a potentially dangerous relationship.

You are someone who can deal with anything if you can deal with an abuser or a toxic relationship. If you can look an abuser in the eye and know that someday, you'll be far away from them, that's more empowering than anything. The day I left my abuser was perhaps the scariest day I ever experienced throughout the entirety of the relationship. My blood ran cold, and I had no idea if they would find me and what they would do if they did. It's so empowering to be able to deal with the trials of abuse while still thinking about what you'll do after you make it out. Your abuser is cold and manipulative, and they will do anything they can to make it so that you never leave. This is their ultimate goal—keep their prey around for as long as possible until they've used up every ounce of spirit in their victim.

Despite this, you have many tools at your disposal to make use of your strengths when you do figure it out. After you address your weaknesses along with your strengths, you can figure out what to do from there based on what your particular situation calls for. That's also where this book comes in handy—there are countless different types of abuse and many different ways that abuse can manifest. Therefore, there are also countless different ways that you can react to that abuse properly and defend yourself against it.

This book is not only to determine how you're being abused and how you can keep yourself from falling for those tricks, but it's also to get you to consider where to go from there. Many books on abuse don't properly take into account the unpredictability of life immediately after a volatile relationship. Being able to look for different ways out, make notes of your abuser's behavior, and have different escape plans available can save you a trouble when you finally make your escape.

If you feel that this book has helped to empower you to grow past your abuse and take matters safely into your own hands, I'd be delighted if you would leave a review to let other people know your story and that they are not alone.

Sources

- Study of Gender and Age in Abusive Relationships: https://www.ncbi.nlm.nih.gov/pmc/articles/PMC3876290/

- Emotional Abuse of Families and Children: https://aifs.gov.au/cfca/publications/emotional-abuse-hidden-form-maltreatment

- Psychological and Emotional Abuse of Children: https://www.nspcc.org.uk/what-is-child-abuse/types-of-abuse/emotional-abuse/

- Common Signs of Emotional Abuse: https://www.healthline.com/health/signs-of-mental-abuse

www.ingramcontent.com/pod-product-compliance
Lightning Source LLC
LaVergne TN
LVHW011012200726
843509LV00011B/1072